PRAISE FOR THIS BOOK

曾經和朋友聊天, 說起我們從小到大學英文的經歷, 我這一代人普遍從小學一年級開始接觸 ABC, 課表上有英文課的記錄直到大學二年級, 長達 14 年之久! 古人寒窗苦讀金榜題名也只需要十年而已啊!

但時間長不是關鍵, "十年寒窗" 后, 初來美國的我們還是會遺憾地遇到一個問題——當我們嘗試用英文去溝通的時候, 美國人常常聽不懂! **我們一直在說的只是中國人眼中的英文, 和美國人眼中的 "中文"。**

爲什麼美國人聽不懂我的英語?! 帶著這個疑問的我如巧合般閱讀了這本書名一致的書。它解答了我的疑問: 因爲你的中文口音! 它也指給我一條出路: 獨特的 66 英語發音體系。

怎麼才叫獨特?

——沒有 "十年寒窗", 三分鐘教你擺脱一些中文口音!

——哪個字母的發音最難? L 第一, R 第二, 你發音正確了嗎?

——放慢語速, 你才能說得更好。

——忘記傳統音標

⋯⋯

何止是獨特呢? 簡直是反传统! 我們哪一個不是藉助音標學英語的? 哪一個英文老師不是告訴我們要夠快才夠熟練夠地道

的? L 怎麼可能最難? 不是 J, Z 或者 M, N 嗎? 三分鐘又能做什麼?

但我照著書中的指導, 嘗試了三分鐘, 然後知道那不是普通的三分鐘! 因為我讀到了作者幾十年的心血凝結, 他用雙腳步行, 卻為我們鋪就了一條 "高速公路"。所以我想說, **如果你的英文是想要講給中國人聽, 那就不要翻開這本書。但如果你的目標是要讓美國人聽得懂, 那就要看看這獨特的 66 發音體系, 讓你的英語 "溜" 起來!**

—Monica Liu - 2013 年 2 月從北京來到美國, 之前在國內從事文字工作 (中文), 先後擔任過新聞記者, 雜誌編輯, 網站策劃。英文是典型的 CHIN-GLISH, 會讀寫不會聽說。

Although I am an American and I cannot read, write, or speak Chinese, I personally endorse Mr. Kenneth Ma's book titled *Why Can't Americans Understand Me?* I have known Mr. Ma for over 30 years both professionally and personally and I knew from the beginning that he had an excellent grasp of English, both written and spoken. When I first knew Mr. Ma, I was Vice President of Sales & Marketing for a U.S. electronics manufacturer and he was an Electronic Engineer. There was an opening for a Far East Sale Manager; the candidate was required to have excellent verbal and written communication skills along with an engineering background.

Mr. Ma was a perfect fit for the position since he had already proven himself as an excellent communicator when dealing with all levels of management. Given his ability to communicate effectively, along with his engineering background, **he was selected over a number of other candidates.**

Over the years I have seen Mr. Ma's English communication skills continue to develop and I know that what he has learned in the business environment will be tremendously helpful to those Chinese who are seeking to improve their English language skills.

—John W. Slumpff
Kenneth Ma's ex-boss and mentor

中国人英语学习常有一种误区，总是以为复杂的，高阶的才能提高自己的水平。觉得自己考过托福，GRE 就代表英语没有问题。实际上在应用时会发现，纵然考过那些很难的考试，还会出现很多交流障碍， 别人不理解，或者自己说不清。这本书告诉我们在英语语音当中的技巧，如何去提高自己的口语发音。

首先，这本书是一个启示。**提醒我们重视最基本的，容易忽略的东西：字母的发音。**大多数的我们很难把英语的 26 字母标准地读一遍。这是我们都会意识到的问题，但是，很少人会重视这个问题。Ken 用很长的篇幅来描述字母的发音。用很多方法和技巧帮助读者学习，训练字母的发音。当你能把这些字母的发音做的很好的时候，英语口语就会有质的提高。你不仅掌握大部分的英语的音节，同时这字母在单词中的拼写。除此之外，Ken 的书中还有许多其他易被忽视的常识，比如注意"尾巴"，一些单词末尾的发音。这些内容已不是传统英语书上的知识，而是告诉读者如何去操作口语这项技能，以及注意事项。

其次，这本书非常有针对性。对以中文为母语的读者在英语口语中常犯的错误，这本书里都有很详细的介绍。中文和英文属于不同的语系，其发音自然也是千差万别。**当我们是对中文的发音很熟悉，很流利时，再开始学习英语自然发音上面会携带已有的中文印记。**Ken 在这本书中就针对中国人常

3

犯的错误进行说明，以及介绍许多改进的训练方法。这些是其他作者里，甚至英语为母语的作者很难做到的。这也使得本书有很大的针对性和应用性。

最后，权威性也是这本书的重要特点。作者 Ken 从小是在中文的环境里长大，一直到大学毕业，然后到美国留学，工作和生活至今。Ken 在家里和工作中都是说英文，所以，他在中文和英文环境里都有丰富的经验。在这本书的写作中他也准备了很长时间，而且他本身也有很多年知识的积累和思考。这本书同时是他对自己英语学习的一次整理和总结。

感谢 Ken 写了一本这么好的书，给我们带来很多有效的学习方法和启示。这本书是华人英语学习的一次革命。

—Steven Qi

Pursuing a Master's degree in Neuroscience, University of Texas at Dallas. Steven came from Huang-Shan, An-Hui province, China. Expecting to graduate in May, 2013.

和大多数的中国学生一样，在我到美国留学之前已经学习了长达 13 年的英语。如果有人问我能不能正确读出 26 个英文字母的发音，或者从 0 数到 10 我一定觉得这是小菜一碟。因为我那 3 岁的小侄女都可以做到，何况我一直英文成绩很优秀还整天美剧不断。然而到美国后，无论在生活还是学习中出现的各种交流障碍让我对自己的英文口语能力产生了深深的怀疑。其实在日常生活中老美讲的口语都用的很简单的单词，而我自己也讲不出什么高级的句子也只能用些简单的话语跟老美交流。然而，很多时候老美讲的几个简单的词，我总是反应不过来是什么；而且有时即便我只对老美说上一两个简单的单词，老美依然一脸迷惑的看着我，在我重复几遍后仍然表示不懂。直到我用尽各种方法解释说明我要表达的那个简单单词，老美才恍然大悟。这时我终于发现，是我的发音出了问题。之前在中国学英语老师总说不要特别在意发音问题,只要老美能听懂就行。要多学些表达方式,这样才能用英语充分表达自己的意思。而现在老美却连我要说的一个简单单词都没听懂,这让我很受伤。让我印象最深的一次,老美问我啥时候入的学,我想说 Fall,然而老美却让我 Say it again. 当时我很想不通,后面系统的学习了这本书才知道,a 的发音和 l 的发音都没有搞对。那这个词你还让老美听什么。作为一个中国人,我们在学习英文的时候自然而然地按照我们所熟悉的音节来发老美的音。我们汉字的发音中没有尾巴,所以我们自然的把几乎英文中所有的尾巴都省略了,每个元音在不同的单词中都会有不同的发音,却又不太有规律,我们就想当然地随便读一个,那你还指望能被老美听懂吗?

从发现自己发音问题导致老美听不懂到系统地学习了这本书,我发现并纠正了自己的各种英语发音的恶习。在这个过程中,我自己以及周围的亲友们都能感受到我的口语交流能力不断提高,从经常跟老美大眼对小眼到流利顺畅愉快的交流。**最开心的是,很多次跟老美交流完,老美都很好奇我在美国呆了多少年了,当我说只有两年时,老美都很惊讶,因为他们觉得我的英文已经比在这边呆很久的中国人好很多了。**其实他们还不知,在我这两年的美国留学中,是最后一年才接触到了这本书和这本书的作者。读了这本书后,根据这本书的指导,我的英语发音才算步入正轨。这本书,一开始就让我的发音在 3 分钟之内超出 90% 的中国人,这一点也不吹牛,我本人有深刻体会。因为我在三分钟之内学会了 kiss 和 keys 的不同发音,而这正是大多数中国人 (90%) 一直没有搞清楚的神秘的 i 的发音,而这个神秘的 "i" 的发音广泛的存在很多英文单词的发音中,一旦搞清楚了,我就几乎改掉了我很多英文单词的错误发音。同时这是一本非常系统的书,读完这本书,我几乎已经横扫了我英语发音的各种错误。书中阐述的六个原则到现在为止都是我提醒自己发音的最佳武器。亲爱的读者们, 如果你现还认为 kiss 和 keys 的发音没有太大差别 或者sh*t 和 sheet 发音基本相同的话。请你马上打开这本书学习神秘的i的发音。千万不要错失这个让你的英文在 3 分钟之内超出 90% 中国同胞的机会。因为我可以负责的告诉你, kiss 和 keys 或者 sh*t 和 sheet 以及其他千万个关于 i 的发音 在老美的发音系统里根本就是千差万别的。要是被你发成一样或者几乎一样的音的话, 那可就小则听不懂闹笑话, 大则老美以为你冒犯他了。

因为在美国留学期间亲身经历了自己和别人由于各种中国口音而不被理解的尴尬和无奈, 也知道要在美国立足, 拥有一口标准或者至少接近标准的美国口音是多么的重要。 然而在众多纷繁的英文口语教学出版物中却没有一本书能够提出并真正解决这个问题。这本书的作者 Ken 用自己 30 多年在美国积累的经验加上他敏锐的听力和极强的模仿能力, 摸索出的这套非常实用的纠正中国人口语的方法, 非常有效地帮助了我, 也希望能够帮到更多的中国人。

—Sijiang Wang
I am from the Yun-Nan province in China. I am pursuing a Master's degree in Accounting at the University of Texas at Dallas and I have been living in Dallas for almost 2 years. March, 2013

"I had a dream…to share my own experience to help Chinese to "re-learn" English speaking". It blew me away when Ken told me about this dream of his.

Ken has carefully and intelligently identified the problems we all have as Chinese learning to speak English. And **he has figured out simple and effective ways to help us improve drastically.**

Now it's on your own determination and effort to experience this breakthrough that will make speaking proper English a reachable goal.

—Sylvia Wan
Ken is a dear friend to my brother and me. We all shared an interest in American rock & roll music and played together in a band while in college back in the 70's. Our friendship has continued for almost 40 years.

Master your English language speaking by focusing on the fundamentals. With decades of experience, research and keen observations, Ken Ma offers important tips and tools for anyone who wants to speak English correctly and be understood without frustration.

—NanPing Chu
Started learning Ken's English pronunciation methods 16 years ago (1997).

我叫 Yeva. 2012 年五月份毕业于 UT Dallas. 现在在一家美国公司工作。

2012 年四月，第一次见到 KEN 是在一个朋友家, 我见到 KEN 的时候他就用英文跟我问好并做自我介绍说他是从台湾过来的, 来美国三十多年了。他做完自我介绍以后我简直就是难以相信眼前这位台湾面孔的人却说着非常标准的英文。这个是非常让我惊讶的，因为我身边的很多华人来美国已经很多年了，可是英文还是带有很浓重的中国口音。我当时顿生好奇。于是那天晚上我们就坐在一起聊英文的学习心得。果然不出所料, Ken 有着很多的英文学习方面的经验。他叫我们要慢慢的说, 很清晰的说, 并且要从 26 个字母开始打基础。那天晚上我跟我的朋友一起跟着 KEN 尝试着纠正自己的发音，很快发现了一些成效。我们很受鼓舞，也很激动，因为似乎在学习英文方面突然找到了一些开窍的感觉。

对于我这个一直呆着浓重的口音说英文的人来说，其实早就放弃了改善英文发音的这个想法了，更不敢奢求像美国人那样去说英文，因为我深刻的体验到了中国人的喉咙与美国人的喉咙之间的巨大差异。我对自己的要求一直都是能够顺畅的表达就够了。可是自从认识 KEN 以后我再也不这样想了，**因为我发现能够把一个语言说的很标准是多么有魅力的一件事情。**

于是我一直都跟 KEN 保持联系，后面就很幸运的成为了他的学生，他从 26 个字母开始教起，更神奇的是 KEN 的学习方法其实是只要学会正确的念 26 个字母，再加上 SLOW, CLEAR, TAIL 就等于成功了一半，接着就是操练。

经过五个月的学习以后我还有我身边的同事都发现我的英文不一样了。我心理非常明白这些都是源自于我很用心的上课和认真体悟的结果。**真的希望有越来越多的人能够在学习英文的道路上少走点弯路。**

—**Yeva Yao**
M.S. University of Texas at Dallas. January, 2013

我認識老馬快三十多年了，他從來沒笑過我的破英文，還常常和我討論中國人學習英文的困難，很佩服他將多年的研究發展出一套簡明的系統，相信大家看這本書時必定會不時會心一笑，深感共鳴。

—**Bruce Tang**
President of Timewave Int'l Corp., Taiwan

我看了您之前发来的两个章节的部分,我感觉很不错,和我以前接触过的英语教材有很大的不同,非常新颖。

对于整个章节的结构来说,我感觉恰到好处。您用几个我们在英语环境中经常遇到但非常困惑的问题来开始整个章节的陈述,比如"为什么美国人听不懂我的英语",或者是"为什么美国人会误解我",这样的问题会让读者对内容产生更多的兴趣,结合他们的自身体会来发现并且解答问题,这样的话给他们的印象也会更加深刻,具体。

同时您用对比的方法让读者了解为什么读音上的一点小误差会让美国人产生很大的误解,比如您用"WU LI"在中文里用不同读音会产生完全不同的意思一样,表现在美国口语里也会遇到同样问题。这样读者就能耐心体会到这样的差别和问题。然后您选出一些中国人平时常误读的英语词汇来提醒读者,遭我们误读的英语发音其实是建立在我们中文发音的基础上的,只有我们中国人自己听得懂,担着并不代表美国人也能听懂。并且您加入您自己的切身体会来提醒读者这一点,让读者意识到我们对自己发音的感觉和美国人听到我们的发音的感觉有着截然的不同,加强读者对学习正确英语发音的必要性,我觉得很好。

最后,我认为这本书的英语还是比较好理解的,在里面我没有遇到什么生词,感觉连贯畅通,整个章节的意思却表达的很好很恰当。这样读者在学习的同时,不仅能够较好的理解内容,**同时又提高了自己的学习英语的自信(因为能够独立的读完一本英语书),**觉得在您的书中找到或者加强了自己学习英语的兴趣,这是非常有效的。

就是关于您发现当时打电话美国朋友不能理解您说 Jim 的例子,我个人在和您聊天当中我认为这是一个非常好的例子,因为我能听到您的发音,并且我们平时确实会把 Jim 中"i"的发音读错。但是在章节中,读者并不能像我们视频聊天中听到您在当时的误读和现在更正后对 Jim 的发音, 所以对他们来说可能这个例子可能没有我们在视频中体现的那样生动。像您在书中举到的其他例子 (比如 David 也会遇到这类的问题), 我觉得都是很好的例子, 但是因为只是文字的陈述, 表现力没有视频中那样生动, 有些可惜。

虽然不像视频中的效果那样, 但是这些例子在书中你的解释已经足以让人体会到发音的区别, 我的意思是, 这都是很好的例子, 如果读者能听到您在这些例子里的发音, 那就更加生动也更具有说服力了。当然这只是我的一些想法, 可能只是我自己的误解, 呵呵。

总体来说, 我觉得这是一本内容切身实际, 结构吸引人, 并且最重要的是对我们学习发音和解决日常口语问题很有帮助的书。

—Roth Zhang
I came from Hang Zhou 杭州, China. Pursuing a Master's Degree in Accounting, University of Texas at Dallas. Expecting to graduate in May, 2013.

I would honestly recommend Ken's book to those who want to make a difference in their own pronunciation. **Especially those Chinese students who learned British pronunciation** when they were in China and find out they don't have a standard British sound nor American sound after they come to the United States. I believe you will have the same amazing experience as I have after you have spent some time on this book.

—Jason Chen - 来自江苏苏州.
Pursuing a Master's Degree (M.S.E.E.) in Electrical Engineering, University of Texas at Dallas. Expecting to graduate in May 2013.

No fancy words or complicated sentence structure, but only hands-on experience and useful tips in the book. **I was surprised when I got to know the name of the book since it has been my question for years.** I couldn't wait to read it and look for the answer. After I went through the whole process of the teaching system which is introduced in the book, I finally found the answer. I felt: "Yes! This is exactly the way native English speakers speak English!" I will definitely recommend this book to every friend of mine who wants to speak real American English and want himself to be understood by Americans.

—**Sisley Wan**
MS in Finance, University of Texas at Dallas. 2012

Why Can't Americans Understand Me?

为什么美国人听不懂我说的英语？

Why Can't Americans Understand Me?

为什么美国人听不懂我说的英语？

A UNIQUE
Teaching System
that Addresses...

一套独特的英语口语发音体系

...English-speaking
COMMUNICATION
CHALLENGES
for Many Chinese

针对许多中国人在英语交流中遇到的尴尬与挑战

Kenneth I. Ma 马一飞

Published by Advantage, Charleston, South Carolina.
Member of Advantage Media Group.

ADVANTAGE is a registered trademark and the Advantage colophon is a trademark of Advantage Media Group, Inc.

Printed in the United States of America.

ISBN: 978-159932-354-1
LCCN: 2013937558

This publication is designed to provide accurate and authoritative information in regard to the subject matter covered. It is sold with the understanding that the publisher is not engaged in rendering legal, accounting, or other professional services. If legal advice or other expert assistance is required, the services of a competent professional person should be sought.

Advantage Media Group is proud to be a part of the Tree Neutral® program. Tree Neutral offsets the number of trees consumed in the production and printing of this book by taking proactive steps such as planting trees in direct proportion to the number of trees used to print books. To learn more about Tree Neutral, please visit **www.treeneutral.com**. To learn more about Advantage's commitment to being a responsible steward of the environment, please visit **www.advantagefamily.com/green**

Advantage Media Group is a publisher of business, self-improvement, and professional development books and online learning. We help entrepreneurs, business leaders, and professionals share their Stories, Passion, and Knowledge to help others Learn & Grow™. Do you have a manuscript or book idea that you would like us to consider for publishing? Please visit **advantagefamily.com** or call **1.866.775.1696**.

TRADEMARK DISCLAIMER

Table of Contents
目录

ANSWERS TO QUESTIONS
问与答

Why Can't Americans Understand My English?
为何美国人听不懂我的英语?

Why Do Americans Misunderstand What I Say?
为何美国人误解我说的英语?

How Can Americans Understand My English?
怎样才能让美国人听懂我的英语?

How Can I Get Rid of My Chinese English Accent?
怎样才能摆脱我的中式英语口音呢?

CHAPTER 2 第二章

53

MORE QUESTIONS AND ANSWERS
更多的问与答

Is This Book for Me?
此书适合我吗?

How Do I Pronounce the Twenty-Six Letters Correctly?
怎样才能把 26 个字母的发音全都发对呢?

How Do I Pick the Right Sound for a Letter in a Word?
怎样从单词里的某个字母选出正确的发音呢?

CHAPTER 3 第三章

61

THE 8 STAGES OF SPEAKING ENGLISH
讲英语的 8 个阶段

Where Are You?
你在哪个阶段呢?

CHAPTER 10 第十章

145

THE CONFUSION COMPOUNDS
混上加混

The Rest of the Vowels: A, E, and U Sounds
剩下的元音: A, E, and U

CHAPTER 11 第十一章

161

THE CHALLENGING SOUNDS
最具挑战性的字母

L (Most Difficult 最难), R (2nd-Most Difficult 次难), and N sounds

CHAPTER 12 第十二章

171

LETTERS STARTING A SOUND
剩下的字母

H, M, Q, X, F, V, J, and G

CHAPTER 13 第十三章

179

THE REMAINING TAIL SOUNDS
剩下的小尾巴

B, C, W, Ch, Gh, Ph, and Sh

真诚的感谢

It has been a dream of mine for more than a decade, to write an English book teaching Chinese how to speak better American English. People laughed at me when I mentioned my dream.

十余年来我一直都怀着一个梦想，梦想有一天能写出一本书，把我在如何让中国人讲出更好的美式英语这个方面的经验，心得和方法写下来。当我与一些人提起我的梦想时，大多数都觉得这不切实际，没有必要，甚至不可能。

The dream is becoming a reality. There are many people I need to thank; without these people's influences and help, a dream is just a dream.

实现梦想的这一天终于到了。有太多人需要感谢，感谢那些影响了我并帮助我把梦想变成现实的人们。

First of all, I need to thank my parents. Without them, I wouldn't be where I am now. Secondly, without my family members' (Juliana, wife; Trevor, son; Justine, daughter) love, support and encouragement, there wouldn't be a book.

首先，感谢我的父母。没有他们，就没有我。其次，感谢我的家庭成员——我的妻子 Juliana，我的孩子 Trevor 和 Justine。没有他们对我的爱，支持和鼓励，就没有这本书。

My special thanks to:

特别谢谢:

Elisabeth Tu who told me 40 years ago "keep on reading the English books even though some of words you don't know the meanings". Thanks for your advice, I have been reading English books ever since.

感谢 Elisabeth Tu (邱学丽), 40 年前她告诉我 "坚持阅读英文书, 即使里面的一些单词你不认识, 那就跳过, 继续读下去"。谢谢你的这句话, 从那以后我阅读英文书一直到现在。

Sylvia Wan who believed in my ability to transfer my knowledge of the nuances of English speaking to other Chinese.

感谢 Sylvia Wan (周新堃), 她一直相信我能把我在英语口语上的知识/经验传达给其他中国人。

My ex-boss Mr. John Slumpff who gave me an opportunity to change my career path from the engineering field to the business field.

感谢 Mr. John Slumpff, 我的前任老板。是他给了我机会, 让我从工程领域转为商业领域, 并因此改变了我以后走的路。

感谢我的初中, 高中和大学的英文老师。是他们教我英语语法, 句子结构, 习语, 并使我一直对学习语言相关的课题感兴趣。

My music playing buddies in college: David Hsieh, Richard Tao, Jeff Chou, Sylvia Wan and Jim Lee. We learned to play and sing American songs without sheet music and lyrics.

感谢大学时代一起玩音乐的朋友们: David Hsieh (谢大为), Richard Tao (陶至诚), Jeff Chou (周新垣), Sylvia Wan (周新

堃) 和 Jim Lee (李功俊)。我们在没有现成的乐谱和歌词下，仍能演奏和演唱英文歌曲。

My first American friends: Jim Cannon and Kevin Kierce and Sheri (Don't know where you are. Hopefully we can reconnect via this book).

感谢我最初认识的一些美国朋友—— Jim Cannon, Kevin Kierce 和 Sheri (抱歉。忘记了她的姓氏)。我们已失去联系，希望藉此书能重新联络到他们。

My students who provided their thoughts and feelings towards English-speaking and gave me challenges on how to teach them better.

感谢我现在的学生们，是他们不断地告诉我他们的想法和感受，并给我挑战如何把他们教的更好。

Many Chinese who indirectly demonstrated their English speaking challenges.

There is a credit run at the end of every movie. The same is true for publishing a book, without these people's talent and help, the book was just a concept.

正如电影制片都会在最后列出演职员名单，本书的制作也同样列出了一份致谢名单——因为每位作者都必须依靠专业团队的智慧和贡献，能把著作从概念变为现实。

The team at Advantage Media Group: Adam Witty and Alison Morse; editors: Denis Boyles, Brooke White and Priscilla Turner—they edited the content into a readable manner, expanded the teaching concepts, corrected my grammatical errors and made concrete my expression of thoughts. The book production team: Kim Hall and Megan Elger, who put the raw materials together into a work of art.

Advantage Media 出版社的团队: 包括 Adam Witty, Alison Morse, 编辑 Denis Boyles, Brooke White 和 Priscilla Turner. 是他们把本书的内容编辑成易读格式, 扩展了我的教学观念, 修正了我的语法错误, 并真实地呈现了我的想法。书本制作团队 Kim Hall 和 Megan Elger, 是他们把原始材料变为艺术品。

English to Chinese translation: Mengmeng Wan—She spent countless hours translating the "not so easy to translate" English content to Chinese and did a great job.

非常出色英译中工作由 Mengmeng Wan (万蒙蒙) 完成。她并花了许多时间把 "并没那么容易翻译的" 英文内容翻译成中文。

Book content reviewers in addition to the publisher's editors: Juliana Tu, my wife and Trevor Ma, my son. Sylvia Wan, David Yen, Gina Lee and Mengmeng Wan—they tirelessly and patiently read through the raw content (both English and Chinese) many times, looking for mistakes and making changes and suggestions.

除了出版公司的编辑们, 我的另一些书评们: 我的妻子 Juliana, 我的孩子 Trevor, 颜新霖, 周新堃, 李冰清和万蒙蒙。他们不辞辛劳并且耐心的把原始内容 (英文和中文) 读了一遍又一遍, 找出错误, 做出改变 并给出建议。

Illustrator: Amanda Loka, who is capable of transferring abstract concepts into simple yet effective illustrations.

插图设计, 所有使写作视觉化, 并为本书增添了 "吸引力" 的绘画都是 Amanda Loka 的杰作。她可以把抽象的概念转化为简单易懂的插图。

Audio and video production: Kirby Penafiel and Richie Wong, who helped to produce related audio and videos.

音频和视频制作：Kirby Penafiel and Richie Wong。他们是摄影机背后的那个人，也是电脑前的那个人，他们拍摄，编辑并制作了所有相关的视频和音频。

Web design and graphics design: Bill and Maggie Stilwell, a very experienced husband and wife team, they have the ability to create beautiful visual effects while developing a complicated accompanying website to compliment the book.

网页设计和平面设计，我交给了 Bill 和 Maggie Stilwell。一对经验丰富的夫妻档。他们可以制作出漂亮的视觉效果，并能开发出与本书相辅相成的复杂的网站。

Lori Ann Robinson, an image consultant who helped Ken to define his personal image statement.

形象顾问 Lori Ann Robinson。她帮助我明确定位我的个人形象。

Intellectual Properties Attorney Robert Louis Finkel who advises me on the legal matters regarding publishing a book and distributing teaching materials.

知识产权律师 Robert Louis Finkel，在本书的出版和教学材料发行相关的法律问题方面的顾问。

Thank you all!

谢谢大家!

I also want to thank my wife, Juliana, who has been teaching and helping me with my English pronunciation, grammar, English related materials, etc. for more than 30 years. Thank you and I love you very much.

环境造就了我们，确实如此。我结发 30 多年的妻子, Juliana, 在家里创造了一个能让我学习语言的环境。没有她，我的英文交流水平会非常有限。谢谢你!

Finally, thank you, the reader. Hopefully I can help you to be rid of unnecessary negative feelings towards English speaking communication.

最后，我衷心的感谢你们，读者朋友们。希望这本书能让你在这门国际性语言的交流上有一个质的飞跃/跨出一大步。

Kenneth I. Ma 马一飞

December, 2012

2012 年 12 月

DIFFERENT WAYS
TO READ THIS BOOK

阅读本书的不同方式

I felt I wrote the same book twice. Initially, this book was written in English. And it was then translated into Chinese. After reading the Chinese translation, I realized some of the English content just can't be translated to Chinese literally. Because of the difference between the Chinese culture and the American culture, some of the Chinese translation won't make sense to Chinese readers who are not familiar with the American language expressions. So I made a lot of changes in the Chinese translation. If you read both the English and the Chinese part and do the comparisons, you will know some of the Chinese content won't match the English content.

我觉得好像把这本书写了两遍。这本书最初是以英文写的，随后被翻译成中文。在读完中文翻译之后，意识到有些英文内容不适宜逐字翻译成中文。由于中美文化的不同，有些中文翻译对于并不熟悉美国语言表达方式的中国读者们来说，是说不通的。于是我在中文翻译上做了很大的改动。如果你把中英文部分读过，对比一下，你会发现有些中文内容和英文内容并不对应。

The book publisher and I tried to determine how to do the book layout with 2 languages; there were many choices, the first half in English, the 2nd half in Chinese. The left side of the page in English, the right side of the page in Chinese, etc. In the end, we have decided to have the English paragraph, then the Chinese translation follows format. It is like watching an American movie with Chinese subtitles. The purpose is to make an easy comparison between the English and the Chinese content.

出版社和我试着决定如何来排版本书的两种语言；我们有许多种选择，前一半英文，后一半中文；书的左页是英文，右页是中文，等等。最后我们决定使用在英文段落之后接着中文翻译这种排版。就像看一部带有中文字幕的美国电影的感觉。目的是便于读者对比中英文内容。

You can read:

- The Chinese portions from the beginning to the end by skipping the English content entirely.
- The English portions from the beginning to the end by skipping the Chinese content entirely.
- Read the content straight through alternating between the English paragraphs and the Chinese paragraphs. The book also serves as a good English reading exercise. If you are not sure of the meaning of the English part, you can find the translation right after the paragraph (most of the time).

你可以这么读：

- 把中文部分从头读到尾，跳过所有的英文内容。
- 把英文部分从头读到尾，跳过所有的中文内容。
- 来回反复的在中英文段落间切换。

本书同时提供了很好的英文阅读练习机会。如果你不确定英文的意思，那就直接去看紧接着的中文翻译。

Hopefully you can read the English portion from the beginning to the end and it should be an easy read for you. I don't know how to use complicated and difficult English words to express my ideas, thoughts; and the purpose of the book is to transfer my knowledge and learning experience to you the easy and understandable way. Not a book to show off my English writing skills and my extensive English vocabulary which I don't have.

你可以从头到尾把英文部分读一遍，希望对你来说很简单。我不知道如何使用复杂难懂的英文词汇来表达我的理念，想法；本书的目的是以简单易懂的方式把我的知识和学习经验转授于你，不是一本炫耀英文写作技巧和运用艰难的英文词汇而著的书。

Let me add a portion of my student's comment here:

这是我的一个学生对本书的评论：

…我认为这本书的英语还是比较好理解的，里面我没有遇到什么生词，觉连贯畅通，整个章节的意思却表达的很好很恰当。这样读者在学习的同时，不仅能够较好的理解内容，同时又提高了自己的学习英语的自信 (因为能够独立的读完一本英语书)…

Hopefully you can say "I finished reading an English book from the beginning to the end".

希望你能说 "我把一本英文书从头到尾读完了"。

Congratulations!

恭喜你!

INTRODUCTION

引言

Have you ever asked yourself one of these questions?

- I have been studying English for years, so why can't Americans understand my English?
- Why do Americans misunderstand the things I say?
- Why are phone interviews so difficult? (This may sound familiar to graduate students who are finishing their studies and have started looking for work in the U.S.)

If you answered with at least one "Yes," or if these topics concern you, then this book MAY BE for you.

- 你是不是尽量避免跟美国人讲英文？
- 跟美国人讲英文时，你是不是感到紧张？不安？忧虑？害怕"丢脸"？是不是变得结巴了？
- 当美国人听不懂你说的英语时，你自己是不是也感到很困惑和惊讶？当你尝试着解释了很多遍，而美国人仍然听不懂你说的英语时，你是不是有挫折感？
- 当美国人误解你说的英语时，你是不是觉得很尴尬？

这些都是作者*以前*亲身的感受。如果以上问题至少有一个你回答"是的"，或者这些话题和你有关，那么这本书也许能让你找到想要的答案和可行的解决方法。

When my American friend, Rex, heard I was writing this book, he was reminded of a book he read years ago, *The Dancing Wu Li Masters*, by Gary Zukav. *Wu li* sounds like a Chinese word to me, but there are many Chinese words that sound like *wu li*. Then Rex told me the book talks about the subject of "modern physics." I immediately guessed *wu li* means *physics* (物理) and I thought I was right. Not really. In the book, *wu li* stands for *physics* (物理) and five other meanings.

当我的一位美国朋友 Rex 听说我要写这本书的时候，他想起他很多年前读过的一本书，是 Gary Zukav 所著的 *The Dancing Wu Li Masters*。*Wu Li* 看上去像是个中文的词语，但是在中文里有很多词语听上去都是 *Wu Li*。Rex 跟我说这本书的主题是讲 "现代物理"。我马上猜 *Wu Li* 就是 *physics* (物理)。并非全对。书中 *Wu Li* 代表 *physics* (物理) 和另外五种意思。

In Mandarin Chinese, every Chinese character can have four spoken tones. That means there are sixteen tone combinations for *wu li* (four tones for the first Chinese character, *wu*, and four tones for the second Chinese character, *li*. Four times four equals sixteen).

在普通话中，每个汉字都有四个声调。对于 *wu li* 这两个汉字，就有至少 16 种不同的声调组合 (第一个字 "*wu*" 有 4 个声调，第二个字 "*li*" 有4个声调。4*4=16)。

From these sixteen possible tones, we can actually derive eighteen possible meanings of *wu li*.

从这 16 种可能的声调组合中，我们实际上找到了 18 个可能代表 *wu li* 的意思。

wu, first tone 一声; *li*, second tone 二声:
乌狸 (1) = dark-colored fox 深色的狐狸

wu, first tone 一声; *li*, third tone 三声:
屋里 (2) = in a room 在屋子里;
乌鳢 (3) = dark-colored fish 深色的鱼

wu, first tone 一声; *li*, fourth tone 四声:
兀立 (4) = stand straight and alone, motionless (for example, a big rock) 独自, 笔直, 静止不动地站立 (比如: 一块大岩石);
污吏 (5) = corrupted officials 腐败的官员

wu, second tone 二声; *li*, third tone 三声:
无理 (6) = unreasonable, nonsense 不合理, 胡闹;
无礼 (7) = rudeness 粗鲁;
吾理 (8) = one's own reasoning 某人的推理

wu, second tone 二声; *li*, fourth tone 四声:
无利 (9) = no profit/benefit 没有获利/好处;
无力 (10) = weakness 虚弱

wu, third tone 三声; *li*, third tone 三声:
五里 (11) = 5 miles 五英里

wu, third tone 三声; *li*, fourth tone 四声:
武力 (12) = military power 军事力量

wu, fourth tone 四声; *li*, third tone 三声:
物理 (13) = physics 物理学;
物理 (事物的道理) (14) = the meaning of something 事物的道理;
雾里 (15) = in a fog 雾里面;
悟理 (16) = to grasp the meaning of something 领悟某事物的道理

wu, fourth tone 四声; *li*, fourth tone 四声:

物力 (17) = material-based power (as opposed to manpower) 物资
力量 (和 "人力" 相对);

悟力 (18) = comprehension, the ability to understand something
理解力, 理解事物的能力

When an American says *wu li*, a Chinese may interpret what he or
she hears as one of eighteen or more possible meanings. Admittedly,
some of the Chinese meanings are rarely used; however, the choices
are still too many at just two Chinese characters, *wu* and *li*.

如果一个美国人说 *wu li* 这两个汉字, 中国人要在 18 个可能
的意思里选一个对的组合来 "猜" 美国人讲的意思。诚然, 其
中一些意思既少用亦难懂, 美国人用这些意思的机会不大。
但是, 剩下的选择仍然很多。

It is often difficult for Americans to learn to speak Mandarin Chinese
in a way that Chinese can understand. Americans have to grasp the
four tones of EACH and EVERY Chinese character. Americans are
not used to these four tones, and that tonality is the fundamental
aspect of speaking Mandarin. If Americans cannot grasp the four
tones of EACH and EVERY Chinese character, then no matter how
hard the Americans try, it is more than likely the Chinese either will
not understand or will misunderstand what the Americans are saying.

对于美国人来说, 中文是一个很难学的语言, 尤其是四声。但
是四声是讲中文的基础。如果美国人讲中文不能掌握每个汉
字的四个声调, 那么无论他们怎么努力的讲, 中国人很有可能
仍然听不懂或者误解美国人在说什么。

The process above also applies to the Chinese speaking American
English. There are twenty-six letters in the English alphabet. At least

one out of five of these letters appears in 99.9% of every English word. These letters are *A, E, I, O* and *U*—the vowels. It would be good if each vowel had only one sound; then the Chinese would get a good start on learning English by focusing on these five letters. Unfortunately, these five vowels can produce at least 30 sounds.

反过来说，英文字母表中有 26 个字母。有五个字母会出现在 99.9% 的单词里。这些字母是 *A, E, I, O* 和 *U*——元音 (母音)。如果每个元音只有一个发音该多好，只要学好这五个音就好了。事非如此，这五个元音至少有 30 种发音。

For example, if a Chinese person knows how to spell a word, but picks a wrong vowel sound, then Americans can hear a simple word like *it* as *eat* or *bit* as *beat*. If the speaker picks a wrong sound for the *E* sound, American listeners will hear *beach* as *bitch* and *sheet* as *sh*t*.

中国人讲英文时，如果选错了元音的发音，美国人很可能会把一个简单的单词 *it* 听成 *eat, bit* 听成 *beat*。如果把 *E* 的发音选错了，那么美国人会把 *beach* 听成 *bitch, sheet* 听成 *sh*t*。

Here are some sample words as pronounced with each one of these 30 sounds. All these words are short and easy to pronounce for many Chinese who have been studying the English language for a while.

A, E, I, O, U 这五个元音的 30 个可能发音举例如下：

The vowel *A* has eight different sounds:

一个单词中有元音 *A*，这个 *A* 至少有 8 种不同的发音：

ape (1); *bad* (2); *bar* (3); *all* (4); *again* (5); *orange* (6); *China* (7); *pea* (8)

If a word has the vowel *A* in it, there are at least eight choices for making the *A* sound in the word.

The vowel *E* has five different sounds:

一个单词中有元音 *E*, 这个*E*至少有 5 种不同的发音:

eat (1); *bed* (2); *interest* (3); *beta* (4); *home* (5)

If a word has the vowel *E* in it, there are at least five choices for making the *E* sound in the word.

The vowel *I* has five different sounds:

一个单词中有元音 *I*, 这个 *I* 至少有 5 种不同的发音:

ice (1); *it, bit, Jim,* or *David* (2); *chief* (3); *mini* (4); *business* (5)

If a word has the vowel *I* in it, there are at least five choices for making the *I* sound in the word.

The vowel *O* has six different sounds

一个单词中有元音 *O*, 这个 *O* 至少有 6 种不同的发音:

oat (1); *Don* (2); *sorry* (3); *love* (4); *woman* (5); *phoenix* (6)

If a word has the vowel *O* in it, there are at least six choices for making the *O* sound in the word.

The vowel *U* has six different sounds

一个单词中有元音 *U*, 这个 *U* 至少有 6 种不同的发音:

you (1); *cut* (2); *blue* (3); *yogurt* (4); *minute* (5); *laugh* (6)

If a word has the vowel *U* in it, there are at least six choices for making the *U* sound in the word.

Now, you can see the chance of picking the right sound to use for a vowel letter in a word is slim. Yes, some sounds are more popular than others. However, there are still too many choices. If you pick a wrong sound for a letter in a word you say, American listeners may not understand you. This is just like how Chinese cannot understand Americans who are speaking Mandarin if the Americans can't say the four tones correctly.

你现在可能体会到，选一个正确的元音发音机会并不大。有些发音会比其他一些发音更常用。但是，选择还是太多。如果你选错了你要说的单词中的字母发音，美国人也许就不能理解你了。这正如中国人不能理解一个不能把四个声调发对的美国人讲中文一样。

We Chinese learn English in order to pass English tests, since English is a standard part of high school and university curricula. We are taught (including me, years ago) to learn English grammar, sentence structure, vocabulary, idioms, and so forth. We assume the more we learn about these subjects, the better our spoken English is. From that perspective, what do we do if we speak a kind of English that Americans either do not understand or do misunderstand? We try harder; we try to convey our meaning in different ways to get Americans to understand us. What happens if Americans still can't? We get frustrated; either we give up on communicating with Americans or we learn more English grammar, more complicated sentence structure, more vocabulary, and more idioms so, we hope, Americans can understand us better.

大部分中国人学英语，是为了通过英语测试，因为英语课是初高中和大学的必修课。老师教我们 (包括多年前的我) 英语语法，句子结构，词汇，习语等等。我们以为这些相关科目学得越多，我们的英语越好。如果我们讲的英语美国人听不懂，我们通常怎么做呢? 我们会试法用别的方式向美国人传达我们的意思。如果美国人仍然听不懂呢? 我们可能会很沮丧，我们也许会放弃避免跟美国人交流，或者我们会去学更多的英语语法，更复杂的句型，更多的词汇，更多的习语，我们*希望藉此*美国人能更容易理解我们。

If you are a native Chinese speaker, have you been thinking the main reason why Americans do not understand or misunderstand you is because of your English pronunciation? Probably not. I did not believe it either. Let me ask you, how hard is it to pronounce the three-letter American name "Jim"? Not hard at all, right? Forty years ago, I was living in Taipei, Taiwan. I made a phone call to my new American friend, Jim, who was spending a summer vacation in Taipei. When his sister picked up the phone, I asked, "May I speak to Jim, please?" At that time, I thought my English was pretty good (compared to that of the other students in the English classes I had taken), and there were no difficult English words to pronounce; I was very confident the person on the receiving end would understand me perfectly even though this was my first time making a phone call to Americans.

你曾想过美国人不理解或者误解你的主要原因是因为你的**英文发音**吗？不信？我以前也不相信。只有三个字母的美国名字 "Jim" 的发音应该不难吧？四十年前，我住在台湾的台北市。我给刚认识的美国朋友 Jim 打了个电话，他正在台北过暑假。他的妹妹接起电话的时候，我说："请问我可以和 Jim 通话吗？"，那时，我认为这个场景的对话老师都教过我们，我也知道每个字的发音。虽然这是我第一次打电话给美国人，我仍然非常自信，我相信电话那头的人一定能听懂我说的英语。

To my total surprise, Jim's sister replied, "Who?" I repeated the same phrase 3 times and she still couldn't understand me. In the end, I had to spell the name *J-I-M* and she finally got it. "You want to talk to

Jim? Let me get him." 'How could this be?' I wondered. My English was perfect, yet she couldn't understand me. I thought about it, and then I noticed her pronunciation of the word *Jim* was very different from my pronunciation of *Jim*.

我完全没想到的是，Jim 的妹妹回答说 "你找谁?"，我把我同样的问语重复了三遍，可她仍然听不懂。最后，我不得不把 J-I-M 这个名字拼出来，她总算懂了。"你找 Jim 是吗? 我帮你叫他"。怎么可能? 挂完电话后，我仔细想了一下，她的英文单词 *Jim* 的发音和我说的 *Jim* 非常不一样，那个音我从来没听过。

Jim killed my arrogance about my ability to speak English.

Jim 抹杀了我对自己英文口语能力的盲目与自大。

Let's go on to a different example. *David* is a popular English male name for Chinese to adopt. Many Chinese pronounce *David* as *day-vee*. Why is *David* pronounced like *day-vee*? There are at least five possible choices for pronouncing the *I* sound in *David*, and most Chinese pick a wrong sound. The sound of the *I* in *David* is the same sound as the *I* in the previous examples: *Jim*, *it*, and *bit*. To highlight another problem with Chinese trying to speak English, the last *D* sound in *David* is often ignored. Americans can mishear "I am *David*" as "I am *navy*" or "I am *devil*."

David 是中国人很常用的男姓英文名。很多中国人把 *David* 说成 *day-V*。为什么 *David* 的发音会像 *day-V*呢? *David* 中的字母 *I*至少有五种发音选择，大部分中国人都选错了*I*的发音。实际上，*David* 中的*I*和之前那些例子: *Jim, it,* 和 *bit* 中的 *I* 发音是一样的。再加上 *David* 最后一个 *D* 的发音总是被忽略，所以 David 就变成了day-V。美国人很可能会把 "I am *David*" 听成 "I am *navy*" (我是海军)或者 "I am *devil.*"(我是恶魔)。

"May I speak to Jim?" and "I am David" are short sentence examples that do not have any complicated English grammar or sentence structure; moreover, all the words are simple one- or two-syllable words. Yet these simple words and simple, short sentences can be easily misunderstood by Americans.

"May I speak to Jim?" 和 "I am David" 都是很短的例句, 都没有复杂的英文语法和句子结构。而且 所有的单词都是简单的, 只有 1 个或 2 个音节的单词。但是这些简单的单词, 简短的句子却仍会很容易被美国人误解。

You might ask, what is the right *I* sound to use when pronouncing *Jim*, *it*, *bit*, and *David*? At the end of Chapter 2, you can learn to pronounce *I* in two minutes or less. It took me 3 months to learn the correct *I* sound forty years ago. Do you have two minutes?

你也许会问, *Jim, it, bit,* 和 *David* 中, *I* 的正确发音到底是什么呢? 在第二章结尾, 你会在 2 分钟或者更短的时间内学会发 I 的音。40 年前, 在没有人教我的情况下, 我花了 3 个月时间才学会 I 的正确发音。你有两分钟的时间吗?

CHAPTER 1

第一章

Answers to Questions

Why Can't Americans Understand My English?

为什么美国人听不懂我说的英语?

Why Do Americans Misunderstand What I Say?

为什么美国人误解我说的英语?

How Can Americans Understand My English?

如何才能让美国人理解我说的英语?

How Can I Get Rid of My Chinese English Accent?

如何才能摆脱我的中式英文口音?

In the Merriam-Webster dictionary, the word *understand* is defined as "to *grasp* the meaning of."

在韦氏字典中，单词"understand"的定义是"理解某事物的意思"。

Relying on certain expectations, Americans understand my English regardless of whether I have a Chinese English accent or not

不论我有没有中式英文口音，在某种期望下，美国人都能听得懂我说的英语

Suppose I am giving my phone number to an American; whether he hears *"fo fi tree"* or *"four five three,"* he will still grasp the meaning of "453." My Chinese English accent (my pronunciation of these numbers in English) is not that critical because Americans expect to hear nothing but some numbers.

假设我要把我的电话号码告诉一位美国人，无论他听到*"fo fi tree"*还是*"four five three"*，他都能理解那是"453"。我的中式英文口音（我说这些数字时的英文发音）并没那么重要，因为美国人想要听到不是别的，只是一些数字。

Likewise, if a conversation is related to an interest rate, whether Americans hear "3 *person*" or "3 *percent*," they will grasp the meaning of 3%.

同样，如果一段对话是有关利率的，无论美国人听到"3 *person*"还是"3 *percent*"，他们都知道是 3% 的意思。

Whether Americans hear *"Sun Q"* or *"Thank you,"* *"U wel-con"* or *"You are welcome,"* they know what I intended to say.

无论美国人听到 *"Sun Q"* 还是 *"Thank you"; "U wel-con"* 还是 *"You are welcome"*。他们都知道我要说什么。

When Americans can hear and grasp the meaning of what I say, Americans do understand my English.

当美国人听到并理解我说的话的意思时，美国人确实能听懂我说的英语。

Americans do not understand or misunderstand my English because I speak Chinese to Americans

美国人听不懂或者误解我说的英文，因为我对美国人说中文

Some Chinese learn how to say an English word by transposing the word into a Chinese-sounding equivalent. Most Americans do not know Mandarin Chinese. If Don is pronounced 当 and Jim is pronounced 近, Hollywood sounds like 好莱坞 and San Diego sounds like 圣地牙哥. Yet Americans' ears do not recognize these 当, 近, 好莱坞 and 圣地牙哥 sounds. **You think you are speaking English to Americans, but you are actually speaking Chinese to Americans.** In such cases, Americans do not understand what you are saying.

有些中国人是通过把英文单词转换到对应的中文来学习这个英文单词的发音。大部分美国人都不懂中文。如果 *Don* 的发音是 "当", *Jim* 的发音是 "近", *Hollywood* 的发音是 "好莱坞", *San Diego* 的发音是 "圣地牙哥"。可是美国人的耳朵听不懂这些 "当"，"近"，"好莱坞" 和 "圣地牙哥" 的发音。你以为你对

美国人讲的是英文，但实际上你在跟美国人讲中文。在这种情况下，美国人不能理解你在说什么。

With my incorrect pronunciation of the twenty-six letters and incorrect selection of English letter sounds, Americans may understand or may misunderstand my English, possibly with unexpected outcomes (embarrassment, anger, outrage, burst into laughter, etc.) that I didn't anticipate

我的 26 个字母的发音不正确，英文字母的发音选择也不正确，美国人也许会理解，也许会误解我说的英语，也许会造成我完全未预料的结果 (尴尬, 生气, 暴怒, 爆笑等等)

Suppose I mean to say, "I like the fresh smell of the bed sheet." However, if I pick the wrong *E* sound for the word *bed* and the word *sheet*, Americans could hear:

假如我想说 "我喜欢床单很清新的味道"。然而, 如果我选错了单词 bed 和 sheet 中E的发音, 美国人会听到:

"I like the fresh smell of the *bed sh*t*" (sh*t on a bed);

"我喜欢床上粪便的味道";

"I like the fresh smell of the *bad sheet*" (a bad sheet of cake, maybe?);

"我喜欢一块坏了的蛋糕的味道";

"I like the fresh smell of the bad sh*t" (?*!@#^?).

"我喜欢臭屎的味道" (?*!@#^?)。

In these cases, Americans grasp the meaning of what they hear, not what I say. If the meaning is not what I intended to say, then Americans either do not understand me or they misunderstand my English.

Americans do not understand my English; my English is incomprehensible
美国人完全听不懂我说的英语

Given any combination of my Chinese accent, my incorrect English letter pronunciation, my selecting the wrong sound for a letter in a word, my speaking Chinese to Americans, and my selection of words to express my thoughts in English (vocabulary, grammar, etc.), the English I speak becomes totally incomprehensible. Americans do not understand what I say.

我的中式英文口音, 不正确的英文字母发音, 单词中的字母选择错误的发音, 对美国人讲中文, 用英文表达想法时所使用的

言语 (词汇, 语法等等), 以上这些任意组合在一起, 都使我讲的英文变得完全令人费解。美国人听不懂我在说什么。

We have discussed the whys. Now, we discuss the hows:

以上提到的是 "Why", 现在我们来讨论 "How":

How can Americans understand my English?

如何才能让美国人理解我说的英语?

How can I get rid of my Chinese English accent?

如何才能摆脱我的中式英文口音?

The short and straight answer to both the above questions is to do the following: 1) pronounce the twenty-six letters (*A-Z*) *correctly*; 2) pick and pronounce the *right* sound for each letter in a word.

以上两个问题直接而简单的答案是: 1) 正确 的发 26 个字母音; 2) 选择单词中的每个字母的正确发音。

We have been taught to work on the more advanced English-language subjects and leave out the basics. How much time did your first English teacher spend in teaching you the pronunciation of all twenty-six letters of the English alphabet *(A – Z)?* Not much, I guess. I do not recall spending that much time learning the alphabet. Most of the English tests I was given were evaluating my comprehension and memorization of grammar, sentence structure, and vocabulary. Speaking English and pronouncing English words were not the focal points of the English tests.

在课堂上, 老师教我们更高级更艰难的英文课题, 而忽略了基础。记得你的第一位英文老师花了多长时间教你英文字母表中 (A-Z) 所有 26 个字母的发音呢? 我不记得我曾花很久的时间去学 26 个字母正确的发音。我所参加过的大部分英语测试都是在评估我对语法, 句型, 和词汇的理解和记忆。英语口语和单词发音并不是英语测试的重点。

Based on my personal observations over the last thirty years, 90% of native Chinese speakers who live in the U.S. cannot pronounce all the English letters correctly and 95% of native Chinese speakers cannot pronounce the numbers *0* through *10* correctly.

根据我过去三十多年的观察, 90% 住在美国的中国人不能把 26 个英文字母的发音发对, 95% 的中国人对英文数字 0 到 10 的发音都不正确。

Curious to know if you fall into the 90% or the top 10%? We offer a free analysis of your English pronunciation of the twenty-six letters (A – Z) and the first eleven numbers (0–10). Submit your letters and numbers pronunciation recording in MP3 format to AtoZ@66English.com; we will let you know if you get all the A to Z letters and all the 0 to 10 numbers right.

想知道你到底属于 90% 还是前 10% 吗? 我们为您提供了免费的分析机会, 来测试你的 26 个字母 (A-Z) 和前 11 个数字 (0-10) 的英文发音。请把你的字母和数字的发音以 MP3 格式录制下来并发送至邮箱 AtoZ@66English.com, 我们会告知你的字母发音是否正确。

Once you have mastered a better pronunciation of these letters, Americans will better understand your spoken English. In addition, your years of work learning English grammar, sentence structure, vocabulary, and idioms will start paying off handsomely.

一旦你能把这些字母的发音发的更好，你花了多年时间努力学习英语语法，句子结构，词汇和习语，就派上了用场，美国人就能更容易理解你讲的英语。

CHAPTER 2

第二章

More Questions and Answers

Is This Book For Me?

这本书适合我吗?

How Do I Pronounce the Twenty-Six Letters Correctly?

如何才能把 26 个字母的发音发正确呢?

How Do I Pick the Right Sound for a Letter in a Word?

如何从单词中的字母选择正确的发音呢?

Is this book FOR me?
这本书适合我吗?

I did mention in the Introduction that this book MAY BE for you. Even if you are Chinese, though, this book is NOT for you if:

- You do not need to speak English to Americans. Many native Chinese speakers live in the U.S. and do not actually need to speak English to live well.

- You firmly believe you can communicate well with Americans and can pronounce all twenty-six letters and most English words correctly.

- You cannot identify or pronounce the twenty-six letters of the English alphabet and cannot read or speak simple English sentences. The teaching system presented here requires basic knowledge of English reading, listening, and speaking.

我在引言部分提过, 这本书*也许*适合你。但是, 如果有以下情况, 那么即使你是中国人, 这本书也许仍不适合你:

- 你不需要跟美国人讲英文。有些中国人虽然生活在美国, 但是实际上他们并不需要讲英文也生活得很好。

- 你坚信你可以跟美国人沟通的很好, 并且你觉得你的 26 个字母和大部分单词的发音全都正确。

- 你不认识英文字母表中的 26 个字母, 或者不会它们的发音。你不会阅读和说一些简单的英语句子。本书的教学体系需要读者具备基本的英语阅读, 听力, 和口语能力。

How do I pronounce the twenty-six letters correctly?
我怎样才能把 26 个字母的发音发正确呢?

The first step to solving any problem is to *acknowledge* that you have a problem.

解决任何问题的第一步 就是先要*认知*问题的存在。

The hardest part is to realize that you have a problem pronouncing the twenty-six letters correctly. I acknowledged my English problem when the other party on a phone call could not understand my pronunciation of *Jim*. If I had not known I had a problem forty years ago, I probably would not have written this book.

40 年前当对方在电话里听不懂我的 *Jim* 的发音时，之前我並未意识到我的英语发音有问题。如果当初我不认知我有英文发音的问题，我今天写不出这本书。

How hard is it to pronounce the twenty-six letters correctly? Of the twenty-six letters *(A – Z)* in the English alphabet, the pronunciation of sixteen letters is new to native-speaking Chinese (see the following table for these 16 new sounds). That means of the twenty-six letters, almost 2 out of each 3 letter sounds are new to us. Usually, Chinese learn these new sounds by referring back to what they already know: Mandarin Chinese sounds. They look for similar, existing Mandarin Chinese sounds with which they can replace these new American English sounds. However, this approach is flawed; because of it, most of us were taught to pronounce these new sounds incorrectly. We spent very little time truly learning how to pronounce English letters correctly. For instance, I was pronouncing *N* as 恩 for years. The hard part is to un-learn and re-learn many of the new sounds.

要把 26 个字母的发音全都发正确, 有多难呢? 英文字母表 (A-Z) 中的 26 个字母里, 有 16 个字母的发音对于中国人来说都是陌生的 (这 16 个字母表请见下一页)。这意味着, 26 个字母中几乎有三分之二的字母音对我们来说都是陌生的。通常, 中国人通过参考已知的东西来学习这些字母: 通过中文的发音。他们去寻找相似的, 已经存在的中文发音来替代这些新的英文发音。然而此方法是有缺陷的, 正因如此我们大多数人学的这些新的字母音都是不正确的。我们真正去学习如何正确的发英文字母的发音的时间少之又少。举例来说, 我很多年来都一直把字母N的发音发成 "恩"。

The purpose of this book and of the 66English_{SM} system I have developed (visit www.66English.com for details) is to make the hard part easier. I have gone through the hard way to learn to pronounce each English letter and word correctly, and I have figured out how to transfer my know-how to you. This way, you do not have to go along the same path I took for many years.

这本书和作者所开发的 66 溜溜英文教学体系的目的是 "变难为易"。我已经在学习每个英文字母和单词的正确发音上经历了一番痛苦挣扎, 我也愿意和已经知晓如何把我的心得转授于你。这样, 你就并不需要再把我经历多年走过的弯路再走一遍。

16 New Sounds For Chinese Speakers
中国人陌生的/不熟悉的16个新发音

A	B	C	D	E	F	G	3
H	I	J	K				3
L	M	N	O	P			3
Q	R	S	T	U	V		4
W	X	Y	Z				3
							16

Out of 26 letters (A-Z), 16 are new for Chinese speakers 16/26 = 62%
26个英文字母中（A-Z），16个字母发音对于中国人来说是陌生的/不熟悉的

Learn to pronounce the mysterious *I* sound in two minutes or less

在两分钟甚至更短时间内，学会神秘的*I*的发音

It took me three months to learn to pronounce the *I* sound and to say words with this *I* sound in them correctly. It also took me many different attempts with my students to figure out how to actually show people how to pronounce *I* correctly and effectively. Here is the free lesson:

1. Say the letter *E* in the alphabet: *E*…
2. Think of how to say the word *yes*. Now say it without the *S* sound at the end: *ye*.
3. Combine the *E* sound and the *ye* sound: *'E'+ye*.

Now, try to pronounce the word *it* with the new *I* sound. Does the word *it* sound different to you?

This is the specific *I* sound that I couldn't pronounce 40 years ago.

Your two minutes are up!

40 年前我花了3个月的时间去学习发 *I* 的音，并学习如何把带有字母 *I* 的单词的发音发正确。我也和我的学生们尝试了不同的方法找出如何正确发 *I* 的音的捷径。

如何**发神秘的 *I* 的发音**?

1. 发字母表中的E的发音: *E*...
2. 发单词 yes 的音。发 yes 不带结尾的 *S* 的音: *ye*
3. 把 *E* 的发音和 *ye* 的发音结合在一起: *'E'+ye*

现在，用新的 *I* 的发音发单词 *it* 的音。是否单词 *it* 的发音听上去不一樣了？

这就是我 40 年前不会发的那个 *I* 的音。两分钟到了！

Once you master this sound, you should be able to pronounce the following words correctly: *it*, *is*, *bit*, *kiss*, *sit*, *David*, and *Jim*…You should also be able to pronounce many more words using the same *I* sound. (See Chapter 9 for the different *I* sounds).

一旦你掌握了这个 *I* 的发音，你应该就能把下面单词的发音发正确了: *it, is, bit, kiss, sit, David,* 和 *Jim…*。你应该也会讲更多带有这个 *I* 音的单词了。(不同的 *I* 的发音请见第 9 章)

Just by pronouncing *I* correctly, you are already pronouncing many English words much better than many Chinese do, and you will find that Americans can understand you better.

只要把 *I* 音发正确，你的很多英文单词的发音就已经比多数中国人好多了，你也会发现美国人能更容易理解你了。

How do I pick the right sound for a letter in a word?

我应该怎样从单词中的字母选择正确的发音呢?

As I mentioned in the Introduction, there are at least 30 sound choices for the five vowels *(A, E, I, O,* and *U)*. There are at least 40 sound choices for the remaining twenty-one consonants. Many of them are airy sounds. For example, the *T* sound has 3 different sounds depending on the word: *eat, patient,* and *depot.*

Therefore, there are at least 70 sounds (30 + 40) associated with the twenty-six letters of the alphabet. Is that surprising to you? I certainly was surprised after I did the analysis.

我在引言中提到 5 个元音 *(A, E, I, O,* 和 *U)* 至少有 30 种发音可供选择。剩下的 21 个辅音,也至少有 40 种发音可供选择,许多辅音都是空气音。比如 *T* 在不同单词中有三种不同发音: *eat, patient* 和 *depot.*

所以,英文字母表中的 26 个字母就有至少 70 种 (30 + 40) 发音。觉得吃惊吗? 在我做完分析之后,我白己也吓了一跳。

To pick the right sound for a letter in a word seems like a daunting task. However, the shocking numbers are not the hardest part. The hardest part is to acknowledge that you often have problems picking the right sounds.

Normally, we start speaking English without giving too much thought to how each word should sound. It does take time to learn to pick the right sound for a letter in a word.

选出一个单词中的某个字母正确的发音好像是蛮难的。其实，难的是你是否愿意去选某个字母正确的发音。

通常我们讲英文的时候，并没有在每个单词应该怎么发音上面想太多，会唸就好，对不对再说。

想学习为单词中的字母选择正确的发音确实需要花点时间。

In Chapter 6, I will show you how to get rid of some of your Chinese English accent instantly—in three minutes or less.

在第 6 章，我会教你如何在三分钟或者更短时间内，即刻摆脱你的一些中式英文口音。

In Chapter 7, I will show you how you can learn to make five new sounds correctly—in two minutes or less.

在第 7 章，我会教你如何在两分钟或者更短时间内学习把 5 个新的字母音发对。

See, it is not that bad. Feel better now? Ready for some more?

其实没有想像的那么难吧。想学习更多吗?

CHAPTER 3

第三章

The 8 Stages of Speaking English

Where Are You?

讲英语的八个阶段，你在哪个阶段呢?

We native Chinese speakers have special difficulty with English. Going from "not speaking English" to "holding an American English conversation with Americans" is an eight-stage process. Here is how it breaks down:

我们土生土长的中国人在学英语上有着特殊的困难之处。从"不讲英语"到"用美语跟美国人对话"，有八个阶段的过程:

WHY CAN'T AMERICANS UNDERSTAND ME?

Are You at Stage 1?

第一阶段

We have studied English for years, but we are afraid to open our mouths to speak the language.

么多年来，我们都在学"哑巴英语"，我们一直都很怕开口讲英语。

When I was a sophomore back in Taiwan, I was at this stage. The Vietnam War was still going on at that time, and many American soldiers were stationed in Taiwan. Near one airbase, in Taichung, were nightclubs where some Filipino bands were playing. One day, my friend and I took a four-hour train ride to visit one of these nightclubs, just to listen to a Filipino band play American songs. After the band finished playing, we took an elevator on our way out of the club. The band members happened to be in the same elevator. I wanted to let them know that they had really played the American songs well; however, I stuttered. I could not come out with a single English word. We smiled at each other. That was it. After we left the club, my friend asked me why I did not say anything to these Filipinos. I said I wanted to talk to them, but no words came out of my mouth.

回溯到我大二在台湾的时候，我正处于这个阶段。那时正值越战时期，许多美军驻扎在台湾。在台中的空军基地隔壁，有很多夜总会，一些菲律宾乐队在里面表演。有一次，我和一位朋友坐了四个小时的火车，专程赶往那个城市的其中一家夜总会，就是为了去聆听菲律宾乐队在那家夜总会演唱美国歌曲。当他们的音乐表演结束后，我们乘电梯离开，正巧菲律宾乐队的成员也在这个电梯里。我真的很想告诉他们，他们演唱美国歌曲真的太精彩了! 然而我却结巴了。我连一个英语单词都说不出来。我们对彼此致以微笑, 仅此而已。离开夜总会以后, 朋友问我为什么对这些菲律宾人一句话都没说。我回答说我很想, 可是嘴巴连一个字也说不出。

You might have heard of a Chinese song called "爱你在心口难開" ("I love you but these words just can't come out—secret admirer's thought") by a Taiwanese singer 鳳飛飛. "爱美在心口难開" ("Love to speak American English, but English words just won't come out") was exactly how I felt when I was in the elevator. The Chinese word 美 was not the English word *beauty*; it was 讲美語, the English word for *Speak American English*.

你可能听过一首中文歌叫做 "爱你在心口难开", 是由台湾歌手凤飞飞演唱的。当我在电梯里的时候, "爱美在心口难开" 正是我的感受。这个汉字 "美" 不是英文里的 "Beauty", 而是 "讲美语" (Speak American English) 的意思。

Are You at Stage 2?

第二阶段

We can memorize and shout out short English sentences.

我们可以记住并讲出英文短句。

Some of us were taught to speak by memorizing short English sentences and speak them over and over, faster and faster, and louder and louder in front of our classmates. This exercise was a great way to build self-confidence, but whether those on the receiving end could understand what we were saying was secondary. This teaches us one-way communication, not English conversation.

有些老师是这么教我们的。老师让我们背诵英文短句，一遍一遍的说，并且是当着别的同学的面。对于建立自信，这是个很好的方法。不管接收方是否理解我们说的英语，是次要的。这只是一种单向交流，而不是英文对话。

Are You at Stage 3?

第三阶段

We can make an English presentation in front of classmates.

我们可以在同学面前做英文陈述。

Some of you may have had the experience of making a presentation in English in front of classmates in various courses you took in high school and/or college. In these cases, your presentation was scripted and memorized. These presentations were one-way communication, not English conversation.

有些人可能有过在高中和/或大学的各种课程中在同学们面前做英文陈述的经历。在这些情况下，你的英文陈述是有演讲稿，并且背好了的。这些陈述只是单向交流，而不是英文对话。

Are You at Stage 4?

第四阶段

We can pass a TOEFL speaking test
(applies to students who study in the U.S.).

对于来美国学习的学生来说: 通过托福口语测试

Before I could come to the U.S. to continue my higher education, I had to pass a TOEFL test. The purpose of the test is to assure admissions staff that foreign students can learn in a typical, U.S.-classroom environment with English speaking teachers or professors. The test evaluates English writing, reading, listening, and speaking skills. Today, I do not remember how I passed the test. I remember that my test scores were not that high and the listening part was extremely difficult for me. I am not sure we had a speaking test at that time.

在我来美国读研究所之前, 我必须通过托福测试。测试的目的是确保外国学生可以跟着讲英文的老师/教授在典型的美国课堂环境中学习。它测试我们的英文写作, 阅读, 听力和口语技巧。我不记得我是怎样通过了测试, 唯一记得的是, 我的分数并没有那么高而且听力部分对我来说相当难。我也不记得当时有没有口语测试。

I also heard that some of the Chinese TOEFL test preparation instructors taught the "speak-fast" method, because the test was designed to present ideas in a timed fashion (say, forty-five seconds). Again, with this method there is no back-and-forth dialogue. This is one-way communication.

有些托福备考讲师会教学生 "讲的快" 这样的方法, 因为这项测试被设定成在有限的时间内 (比如, 45 秒钟内) 陈述想法的模式。同样，这种方式并没有一来一回的对话，这也是单向交流。

Are You at Stage 5?

第五阶段

**We speak Chinese to other Chinese,
but occasionally use English words.**

我们与其他中国人讲中文，偶尔夹杂一些英文单词。

What I am describing here is two-way communication. Two native Chinese speakers usually communicate in Chinese between themselves, sometimes throwing in a few English words. Usually, these are English words (such as names of places) that do not have Chinese translated equivalents: for example, the Galleria Mall in Dallas or the Staples Center in Los Angeles. If the names include commonly used, Chinese translated equivalents, we generally prefer using these words (such as "星巴克" for the name *Starbucks*, where "星" stands for *star*). It took me a while to see the relationship between the Chinese letter "星" and the English word star, or to see "巨無霸" or "大麥克" as equivalent to the word *Big Mac*. At this stage, some of us feel our English speaking is quite alright: other Chinese understand the English words we say. I was at this stage until I encountered an American.

这是一个双向的沟通。两个中国人用中文交流，有时夹杂一些英文单词在里面。有些美国的地名我们没有对应的中文翻译名字。例如，达拉斯的 Galleria Mall，洛杉矶的 Staples Center。如果有常用的中文翻译名，我们喜欢用中文名。比如，"星巴克" 是 "Starbucks"。我花了一些时间才理解汉字

"星"和英文字"star"之间的关系，中文"巨无霸"或"大麦克"与"Big Mac"间的关系。在这个阶段，有些人觉得英文口语相当好，别的中国人理解我们说的英文单词。我在高中与大学时，停留在这个阶段（那时还没有 Starbucks, Big Mac),直到我开始与美国人讲话。

Are You at Stage 6?

第六阶段

We speak Chinese English to Americans while using broken communication and guessing at others' meanings.

我们跟美国人讲中式英语 —— 支离破碎的表达，互相猜测对方的意思

If you live or study in the U.S., sooner or later you will speak English to an American. Perhaps you will speak to a store clerk, a non-Chinese restaurant waiter/waitress, a job interviewer, or a police officer. In turn, many Americans now live in places such as China, Hong Kong or Taiwan so you may have had a chance to speak to them in English.

如果你住在美国或在美国学习，迟早你会跟美国人讲英语。不论是跟店员，跟非中国人的服务生/女服务生，跟面试官，还是跟警官等等。目前也有很多美国人住在中国，你也会有机会跟他们讲英语。

At this stage, Chinese speakers can also be understood in context. For example, when the 2012 Olympics were held in London, whether we said "奥林匹克," "*Olympee*," "*Olympic*," "*Olympics*," or "the *Olympics*," Americans would understand to what we were referring.

2012 年奥运会几周前刚在伦敦举办，不管当时我们说"奥林匹克"，"Olympee"，"Olympic"还是"Olympics"，美国人都会理解我们指的是什么。

Are You at Stage 7?

We can hold "Chinese English" conversations with Americans.

我们用中式英语跟美国人对话。

We might have lived in the U.S. for a while, and we might even work for an American firm with colleagues who speak English. We speak Chinese English with better English pronunciation, and we listen, reply to statements, and ask and answer questions in conversations with American coworkers. This two-way communication is limited to job-related topics or specific areas, such as sports or music.

我们可能已经在美国住了一段时间，我们在一个美国公司工作，而且我们的同事都讲英语。我们用更好的英语发音讲中式英语，同时我们听，回复，问和回答美国同事的问题等等。一个双向交流在有限的基础上完成了。谈话的内容限制在工作相关或者特定话题上，比如运动，音乐等等。

Are you at Stage 8?

We can hold American English conversations with Americans.

我们可以用美式英语跟美国人交谈。

At this stage, both parties share back-and-forth communication and can understand each other 100% or near 100% of the time. Clear English pronunciation is essential at this stage.

双方之间有一个来回往复的交流，双方都可以几乎 100% 的理解对方。清晰的英文发音在此阶段是基本要素。

Which stage do you think you have achieved? Are you content to remain at that stage? Would you like to move up to the next stage? Read on.

你目前在哪个阶段？你对自己所处的阶段满意吗？你想进步到下一个阶段吗？请继续读下去。

"Chinese English" is mentioned throughout the entire book; it refers to English spoken by native Chinese speakers. Due to the vast differences in Chinese dialects and in the English language-learning system taught in China, the English spoken by native Chinese speakers differs. Each person's language has its own tones and accents. Sometimes it can be understood by Americans, sometimes not.

本书中常提到 "中式英语"。它是指中国人讲的英语。由于语言间的巨大差异和中国的英文教学系统，中国人讲出的英语有着他自己独特的声调，口音。有时美国人能理解，有时却不能。

CHAPTER 4

第四章

Myths About Speaking English

关于讲英文的一些迷思

MYTH:

Speaking English fast equals speaking English well.

迷思: 英文讲得快等于英文讲的好.

In a totally Chinese-speaking environment, if we hear somebody speaking English very quickly, we tend to think she speaks English very well. We might have no idea what she is saying, but we recognize the English sounds and know she is speaking English. "Wow," we think, "her English is very good."

在一个完全是中文的环境里, 如果我们听到有人英文说的非常快, 我们往往认为他或她说的英语非常好. 我们可能不知道他在讲什么, 但我们可以肯定那不是中文, 而是英文. "哇! 天哪! 她的英语真好!"

If you talk to your American professors or work in an American company, you might believe speaking English slowly makes you appear uncomfortable or seem unintelligent. When choosing

71

between "speak slower but clearer English" and "speak faster but unclear English," most English listeners prefer "speak slower but clearer English." Resist the temptation to speak quickly.

如果你与美国教授谈话或在一个美国公司工作, 你可能觉得英文讲的慢会让你感觉不舒服, 或者让他人觉得自己不够聪明。在讲的慢而清楚和讲得快而含糊两者中, 慢而清楚远胜于快而含糊.

In my English classes, we speak English almost 100% of the time. Inevitably, each student starts speaking English fast—much faster than the rate at which I speak. I remind them to slow down. By the end of the class, they speak much better because they are speaking more slowly.

在我的英文课堂中, 我们几乎 100% 的时间讲英文。每个学生的英文都比我讲英文的速度快多了。我提醒他们放慢速度, 当他们讲的速度放慢下來, 他们的英文发音就好多了。

MYTH:
The fancier the word, the better the English.
迷思: 用詞越花俏, 知道越多單詞, 英語就越好.

The traditional English learning system (in China and Taiwan) teaches people to write and speak using fancy words. Teachers encourage students to memorize words by going through an English dictionary and trying to learn, say, ten words a day. Of course, it is good to expand your English vocabulary; doing so helps your reading skills tremendously.

However, people judge your English by listening to you speak and by reading your written materials, such as e-mails. Typically, they do not judge you by how well you read.

傳統的英文教學系統教我們用華麗的辭藻書寫和說。我們被鼓勵著通過查字典來記單詞，或者試著每天記住 10 個單詞。但我認為 "交流遠遠比學習更多花俏的單詞更重要"。所以，我們可能知道很多的單詞，但卻不會這些單詞的正確發音。當寫作的時候，我們把這些華麗的單詞堆砌在一起放在寫作中，尤其是在研究生的報告，論文和畢業論文的寫作中。這些報告，論文与畢業論文的寫作中，使用正確的單詞 (而不是花俏的單詞)，句子結構和語法，遠遠比丟出花哨的單詞更重要。

As of 2009, an estimated 307 million people lived in the United States. 24% of that number were eighteen years old or younger, making the total adult population about 228 million people. Of that number, over 27 million adults (12%) could not read. An additional 46 million (21%) were so-called functionally illiterate or marginally literate. In other words, in 2009 one out of every three adult Americans lacked the skill required to be satisfactorily literate in today's society. The average American, I have read, has a fifth-grade level of reading comprehension. Now, we are talking about Americans; we have not added the immigrants. So many immigrants from all over the world are here in America. What about their English comprehension levels?

My point here is, why use fancy words if many Americans, not to mention immigrants, will not understand what you are saying? That goes for both speaking and writing.

截至 2009 年，美國總人數為 3 億零 700 萬。其中 24% 的人為 18 歲及以下，成年人總數估計為 2 億 2800 萬。超過 2700 萬 (12%) 的成年人不會閱讀! 另外的 4600 萬 (21%) 就

是所謂的 "功能性文盲" 或者 "邊緣文盲"。這意味著, 每三個成年美國人中就有一人缺乏當今社會所必需的令人滿意的文化程度。我曾讀到美國人的平均水平是小学五年級的閱讀理解能力。我們現在討論的是美國人, 還沒把移民算進來。這裡有許多來自世界各地的移民, 他們的英文理解水平怎樣呢?

所以無論是說還是寫, 如果大部份美國人都不能理解我們的話, 更別提移民了。爲什麼還要用花俏的單詞呢?

TO STUDENTS WHO ARE PURSUING
GRADUATE STUDIES IN THE U.S.

Do you need to write graduate school papers, reports, or your thesis? You might think, "This is a grad-school paper, it is better to use more sophisticated words (fancy words) in my paper to show I am highly educated." To me, the use of correct (not fancy) words, correct sentence structure, and correct grammar is much more important than throwing fancy words in your paper. Other interested parties need to be able to be read and understand your paper; you do not need to show off your ability to use fancy words.

對於想來美國讀研的學生或者正在美國讀研的學生:

你需要写研究生论文, 报告, 或者毕业论文吗? 你也许会想 "这毕竟是研究生论文, 为了能显示出我是受过高等教育的, 最好在我的论文中使用一些更复杂的单词 (花俏华丽的单词)"。 对我来说, 在你的论文中使用正确的单词, 正确的句子结构和正确的语法 远比堆砌花俏华丽的单词更为重要。论文审核人需要能阅读和理解你的论文内容。不需要炫耀你会用华丽词汇的能力。

Before I came to the U.S. to study, I passed my GRE test. I do not recall any of the GRE words I learned for the test, because I do not need to use these words in daily life. Since I do not use them, I forgot them.

爲了來美國讀研, 必須通過 GRE 或者 GMAT 考試。這兩個考試測試了英語詞彙量。爲了通過考試, 我們去背誦大量的花俏的單詞。當然, 記住這些單詞是件好事。但是考試過後, 我們在日常生活中基本用不上他們, 然後我們就忘記了這些單詞。

MYTH:

Native Chinese speakers who live in the U.S. speak English better than those who live in places such as China, Hong Kong, Singapore or Taiwan.

迷思: 去而且住在美國的中國人, 講的英文比住在中國和台灣的人更好。

Chinese who live in these places and have never been to the U.S. make this assumption. However, this assumption does not necessarily reflect the truth.

從來沒來過美國的中國人常會有這種假設。然而, 未必如此。

When I came to the U.S. in the '70s, very few Chinese lived in Los Angeles. During my first semester, I lived in a dorm and had two

American roommates, neither of whom spoke Chinese. I was forced to speak English. If I wanted to go to a Chinese market to get Chinese groceries, I had to get a ride with some other Chinese students to Chinatown, which was a twenty-minute drive from the campus.

當我 70 年代來到這裡的時候，住在洛杉磯的中國人沒有那麼多。第一個學期我住在學校宿舍，有兩個美國室友。他倆都不會講中文，於是我被迫講更多的英文。如果我想去中國超市，我必須找那些有車的中國同學，搭他們的車去距離學校開車 20 分鐘路程的中國城。

Things have changed dramatically in the last 10 years. Many native Chinese speakers who live in big cities (Los Angeles, San Francisco, Dallas, Chicago, and New York, etc.) can get by very well without speaking a word of English. They can take advantage of Chinese supermarkets, doctors, dentists, optometrists, pharmacists, bakeries, restaurants, hair salons, car insurance agencies, airport transportation services, real estate agents, newspapers, TV channels, and so forth.

然而在近十年中，情況發生了戲劇性的變化。許多住在洛杉矶的中國人，可以不用講任何英文而過的非常好。這裡有中國超市，中國醫生，牙醫，驗光配鏡師，藥劑師，麵包店，餐館，車險代理行，中文機場接送服務，中國房產中介，中文報紙，中文電視頻道等等。

MYTH:
The newcomers speak better English than the old comers.

迷思: 新來的人英文比以前來的人英文講的好

The above might seem like a valid assumption, given the wealth of available resources, such as the Internet; websites like YouTube and Youku; pocket dictionaries and online dictionaries; more American teachers teaching English in these places (China, Hong Kong, Taiwan); and children learning English in elementary schools. However, does this new generation of native Chinese, people who have access to all this technology and more exposure to English speakers, really speak better English than the native Chinese speakers who have lived in the U.S. for a decade?

一些高科技比如 因特網, Youtube, 優酷網, 電子詞典, 在線詞典; 越來越多美國人去中國教英文; 孩子從小學就開始學英文等等。新一代的中國人, 在來美國之前就有了這些高科技工具的幫助, 並且有更多機會講英文。他们比那些 10 多年前就來美國的中國人英文講的好嗎?

The answer really depends on where the latter live in the U.S. For example, if a newcomer moves to Kansas City, an area where very few Chinese live, then yes, it is possible that this newcomer's English skills will be better than that of those old comers who live in Los Angeles and do not need to speak English at all.

這一點取決於你所處的地方。如果呆在少有中國人居住的堪薩斯城, 是很有可能。相比很早前就來到洛杉磯而根本不需要講英語的人, 新來的人的英語講得更好。

In contrast, the old comers might know more English words in reference to local places, street names, city names, and people than the newcomers because they have lived in their respective areas longer. In Chapter 5, we will discuss the importance of living in an environment in relation to improving our English.

早前來的人可能比新來者知道更多的有關本地地名，街名，城市名和人物名的英文單詞，因為他們住在這裡更久。在第五章，我們會討論生活環境的重要性。

Much also depends on how old foreign students/immigrants are when they come to live in the U.S. The earlier—say, before or during the early teen years—the better. For some reason, it is easier for young kids and young teens to pick up a language than it is for older people. My relatives are a good example of this. My aunt and her four sons immigrated to the U.S. when my four cousins were in their teens, and all my cousins speak English much better than I do. My parents moved to Los Angeles when they were in their 60s; they spoke little to no English before they came over to the U.S. After they settled down in Los Angeles, their English speaking improved very little over the years.

當然，何時來美國的 "年齡" 也很有關係。越早，比如青少年早期或更早，英语就越好。幼童和少年更容易學會一門語言。我的親戚正好是個好例子。我的阿姨和她 4 個兒子 (我的表弟們) 移民到美國并搬到了洛杉磯。当时，我 4 個表弟都是在少年時期，他們的英文都比我說的好多了。我父母在他們 60 多歲的時候搬到了洛杉磯，在來美國前他們沒說過英文。历年来，他們在說英語這個方面水平幾乎沒有提高。

MYTH:

American born speakers are better English teachers.

迷思: 母語為美語的美国人会是更好的英文老師。

Yes and no. Some American teachers are linguists who really know their materials and are excellent teachers. However, as I mentioned earlier, even though more Chinese are studying English and starting to do so at a much younger age, I have not noticed any appreciable improvements in their English speaking. While they might be good English teachers, perhaps their teaching emphasizes reading, writing, and listening skills over speaking. Perhaps the teachers just accept "Chinese English" speaking. I do not know.

亦对亦不对。有些美國老師是語言学家，真正瞭解他們的专科，他們应该是優秀的老師。但是 正如我先前提過的，雖然越來越多的中國人更早的就開始學習英文；国内大城市有许多教英语的外国老师，也许这些老师把教学重点放在阅读，写作和听力技巧上，而不是口语方面。也许这些外国老师能接受学生的"中式英文"口语。可是我並未感觉一般中國人的英语口语能力有顯著地提高。

I am currently teaching some graduate students, all of whom are from China, to speak American English. Through reading their e-mails, I can tell their English writing skills are very good compared to my own writing when I was in graduate school. Those teachers who teach English writing in China have done an excellent job teaching English writing to these students.

我现在正在教一些住在美国的研究生 (他们全部来自中国) 讲美式英文。他们的英文写作水平比我当时研究生学习阶段的水平相比好很多。我们常通过电子邮件沟通，从和这些学生的邮件交流中看出来，那些在中国教英语写作的教师，教的非常好。

An estimated 150,000 students from China and 25,000 students from Taiwan came to the U.S. to study in 2011; to get here, most of them have passed their TOEFL, GRE, and/or GMAT tests. Those who have taught these native Chinese to pass such different English tests have done their jobs right.

2011 年, 大約有 15 萬從中國來的留學生來美国留学。大都需要通過託福考試, 那些英語老師在教他們如何通過不同的英語測試上面做得非常好。否則這些留學生不能通過託福考試, 也来不了美國。

If someone is Caucasian and speaks English, others assume he or she must be a good English teacher—but that is questionable. It is likely most of us have experienced a teacher or professor who is an expert in his field and knows his stuff down pat but just cannot transfer his knowledge to his students. A person's knowledge of how to speak English does not mean he or she can teach native Chinese speakers how to speak the way Americans speak.

只是因為某些人是美國人并講英文, 就假設他或她一定是個很好的英文老師的想法是令人質疑的。

我們都有過這樣的經歷, 一位在他的領域是專家的老師/教授, 他精通他的東西, 然而他不见得能把他的知識/經驗傳授給他的學生。只因為一個美国人懂得怎麼講英文, 不代表這個人就可以教本土的中國人像美國人一樣說英文。

MYTH:

**Does Ken (this book's author) speak just like
a native American speaker without any accent?**

迷思: Ken (本人, 作者) 英文講的就像本土的美國人一樣好而
且沒有任何口音嗎?

We take the word *accent* for granted, and its meaning can be broad. Depending on the person with whom I speak, I get different answers to the above question: some people hear no accent at all, some hear a very minor accent, some a bit more accent, and so forth. I have lived in the L.A. area ever since I came to the U.S., so I might have a California accent. If I had been living in Mississippi, I might have a Mississippi accent. The same is true for those living in Texas or in New York—each place produces different regional accents.

"口音" 這個詞的意思很廣。取決於我說話的對象，有些人说我完全沒有口音，非常少的口音，一些口音等等。

我來到美國后，一直住在洛杉磯地區，我可能有加州口音。如果我住在密西西比，我可能有密西西比口音。德州和紐約也有不同地區的口音。

Here is my assessment about my own English speaking: I make an effort to pronounce English words as accurately as possible. I have noticed that when I speak more quickly, my pronunciation becomes less accurate. There are still some words with which I am unfamiliar, and I may pronounce them incorrectly. However, I believe my concentration on proper English grammar, vocabulary, correct word usage, and sentence structure has helped me. I will never speak 100% like a native American speaker. I came to the U.S. when I was twenty-six years old, and I have deep roots to Chinese culture and language. I believe I communicate pretty well in general; in conversation, I understand what the other party is saying and the other party understands what I am saying, and we do not have to guess at each other's meaning. I get into trouble if I participate in a conversation regarding subjects with which I am not familiar, such as American football games, certain medical terms, procedures, and so forth.

這是我對我自己講的英文的評定。我一直努力嘗試讓英文單詞的發音盡可能的準確。同時我也注意到，當我講的快的時候，我的發音就會沒有那麼準確。有些單詞我不認識，我可能就會讀錯。我認為英語語法，詞彙，單詞的使用和句子結構這些所有組合在一起 造成了我現在講話的方式。我永遠沒辦法講的 100% 像個地道的美國人，因為我有著根深蒂固的 (我來美國的時候是 26 歲) 中國文化和中國語言。我認為總體來說，我可以与美国人交流的非常好，我理解對方說的話，對方也理解我在說什麼，而不用去猜測雙方的意思。如果我參與談論我不熟悉的話題时，我也會遇到困难。比如說美式足球比賽，某些醫學術語，治疗過程等等。

The bottom line is, you do not need to have flawless, unaccented speech, which is regionally subjective anyway. You just want to be understood by Americans without them having to guess at what you are saying.

達到完美的，沒有口音的言語—— 這點帶著地域性的主觀——是不需要的。**需要的是讓美國人不用通過猜測就理解我們。**

CHAPTER 5

第五章

A Unique Approach in Speaking the English that Americans Will Understand

讲让美国人听得懂的英语

Introducing the 66English$_{SM}$ System

介绍 "溜溜英语体系"

I was taught to speak English the traditional way, which did not work for me. Thus, I had to un-learn what I was taught and then relearn the hard way—by listening to Americans very carefully and copying what I heard. By using this method, I finally learned to speak American English. Once in a while, someone would mention to me that he could not understand the words I said, so I would then go back to figure out why he could not understand me and try to correct it. However, it was a very slow process because I had no real teachers. I was self-taught.

我在传统英语教学环境下学的英语，碰上了美国人，在许多情况下还不管用。如何管用呢？在没有人，老师指点的环境下，只有用最笨的方法来自学——仔细听美国人是怎么说的，然后模仿我所听到的。这个过程相当缓慢。

I had no one who could point out my errors or correct my mistakes until I got married. Juliana, my wife, is Chinese, but she traveled with her family to different countries at a young age and her first language was English. During all the years we have been together, she has been helping me correct my English pronunciation and grammar.

从 1972 年到我结婚之前 (1979)，几乎没有人自动地指出我的发音错误，也没人纠正我的发音错误。我的妻子 Juliana 是中国人，但她从小跟随她的家人旅居各国，所以她的母语是英文，她的普通话也说的相当不错。我们结婚这些年里，她一直帮我纠正我的英语发音和语法。

How can I transfer my know-how to you with minimal effort on your part?

Let me introduce the 66English System. The system is designed to accomplish the knowledge and experience transfer so that you do not have to go through the same painful learning process I went through.

我如何能事半功倍的把我的心得转授于你呢？我研发出 "溜溜英语体系" 就是为了把我的知识和经验转授于你，你不用再经历一番我当时痛苦的学习过程。

Use your six senses (the first number "6" of 66English) and apply the six principles (the second number "6" of 66English) to learn. This is the foundation of the 66English System.

"溜溜英语体系" 的基础建立在如何运用 6 个感官 ("66 英语"的第一个 "6") 与如何运用 6 种原则 ("66 英语"的第二个 "6")。

Make Sense - The Six Senses
六官

SENSE 1: YOUR BRAIN
第 1 官：你的大脑

You might have hit a roadblock with the traditional way of learning English. You will not go very far if you keep trying the same methods. The 66English System is very different from other methods to which you may have been accustomed to. In order to adapt to the new system, you need to think differently. You will get much better and faster results if the new concepts sound sensible and the systematic approaches make "sense" (that's a pun) to you.

也许你在传统的英语学习之路上遇到了障碍。如果你还坚持使用同样的方法，你的进步也许不会很大。"溜溜英语体系"和你所习惯的方法有很大的不同。为了能适应新的方法，你需要换一种思考方式。如果新的理念对你来说"说得通"，你就会得到更好更快的效果。

SENSES 2 AND 3: YOUR MOUTH AND TONGUE
第 2 官和第 3 官：你的嘴巴和舌头

Have you had this experience? You develop a canker sore in your mouth, which hurts, so you talk less. When you do have to talk, you adjust your mouth muscles and your tongue to avoid the sore, and so you sound different.

你曾有过这种经历吗？你得了口腔溃疡，它很疼，所以你少说话。当你不得不开口说话的时候，你就调整嘴部肌肉和舌头来避免碰到溃疡处，于是你的发音变了。

Using the combination of the mouth's muscles and tongue movements to make long, expressive American English sounds is foreign to Chinese speakers. We were not taught to speak English by using long, expressive sounds; instead, we automatically use our mouth muscles and tongues to speak English with short, abrupt sounds.

对中国人来说，把嘴部肌肉和舌头的运动组合在一起，发出长而富有表现力的美式英文发音，是很不自然的。我们没有学着通过发长而富有表现力的发音来说英语，我们无意识的用嘴部肌肉和舌头发出短促的英文音。

SENSE 4: YOUR EARS
第 4 官：你的耳朵

Babies do not learn to speak a language by learning an alphabet first. Instead, a baby copies sounds by listening to his or her mother talking. The baby starts mimicking the mother by using short, syllabic sounds, such as *mama*.

婴儿们并不是通过先学会字母表而学会说话的。婴儿会重复他所听到的妈妈讲的话。他们是通过使用短的，重复的发音来开始模仿妈妈的讲话，比如：*mama*。

If your ears are used to Chinese English sounds, you will automatically copy these sounds and your English will sound like Chinese English.

如果你的耳朵习惯了中式英文发音，那么你会不自觉地就模仿这些发音，你的英文听上去就像中式英文。

Using your ears is an important part of the 66English System. I will show you how to listen to the subtle differences between sounds that most Chinese ignore or fail to catch. Once you hear them, you can differentiate among these sounds and learn to copy American English sounds. This way, your spoken English will sound more like American English.

在"溜溜英语体系"中，运用你的耳朵是非常重要的一个部分。我会教你如何听出发音之间的细微差别，这些差别是大多数中国人都会忽略或者听不出来的。一旦你听出了这些差别，你就会区别这些不同的发音，并学会模仿美式英文发音了。这样，你的英文口语听上去就更像美式英文了。

SENSE 5: YOUR EYES
第 5 官：你的眼睛

We read English words, phrases, sentences, books, and so forth with our eyes. Normally, we do not watch someone's mouth shape and tongue movements (if we can) when that person speaks because it is considered impolite. Using your eyes is an important part of the 66English System.

我们通过眼睛来阅读英文单词，词组，句子和书等等。通常当一个人讲话时，我们不会去盯着那个人的口型和舌头的运动，因为这是不礼貌的。在"溜溜英语体系"中，运用你的眼睛也是一个很重要的部分。

A sound is produced by a combination of mouth shape and tongue movements. If you can see and copy the mouth and tongue movements when someone produces the sound, you have a much better chance of producing the same sound. If an American's mouth shape and tongue movements are different from yours, then the sounds that come from your mouth will be different. In other words, if you use the wrong mouth shape and tongue location, you will produce a wrong sound.

声音是由空气，口型和舌头运动组合在一起而产生的。当一个人发音的时候，如果你能看到并模仿他的嘴巴和舌头的运动，你就更容易发出同样的一个音。如果一个美国人的口型和舌头运动跟你的不一样，那么从你嘴巴里发出的音就不同。换句话说，如果你的口型和舌头位置不对，你的发音就不对。就这么简单。

This is the shortcoming of a pocket or online dictionary. In the case of the latter, you can only hear a word's pronunciation by clicking the speaker icon next to the word. You may or may not be able to duplicate the sound just by listening to the pronunciation, since you cannot see how the sound is produced by the combination of mouth shape and tongue movements.

袖珍字典和在线词典都存在一个缺陷。就在线词典来说，你可以通过点击单词旁边的扬声器符号，"听到"单词的发音。仅仅通过听这个发音，你也许可以，也许不能复制出这个发音，因为你"看不到"这个发音是如何通过口型和舌头运动组合在一起发出来的。

SENSE 6: YOUR HANDS
第 6 官：你的手势

Hand gestures (by the way, *G*, the first letter of the word *gesture*, sounds like *J*, not *G*) are powerful communication tools. Two people who speak two different languages can use hand gestures (比手划脚) to communicate. Babies can communicate with parents with hand gestures; people can use hand gestures to communicate with animals.

手势 (顺便一提, 单词 *gesture* (手势) 中的第一个字母 *G,* 发音像 *J,* 而不是 *G)* 是一个非常有用的交流工具。两个讲着不同语言的人, 可以用手势交流; 婴儿可以通过手势跟父母交流; 人类可以通过手势跟动物交流。

Why not use hand gestures to help us improve our pronunciation? I have used hand gestures with my students to achieve great results.

为什么不借用手势来帮助我们改善我们的发音呢? 我曾通过跟我的学生们使用手势而取得了显著的效果。

Out of the six senses, which is the most important? Your brain. The rest of the senses will work for you only if the concepts of this system make sense to you.

六官之中, 哪个最重要呢? 第 1 官: 你的大脑。只有当你能理解和接受 "溜溜英语体系" 的概念, 剩下的五官才会对你起作用。

The Six Principles
六原则

If you get stuck while improving English speaking skills, it is possible that you forgot to apply one or more of the principles. Here are the six principles:

如果你在提高英文口语技巧的过程中遇到障碍停滞不前, 那么很有可能是因为你没有应用其中一个或多个原则。以下是六原则:

PRINCIPLE 1

Do not replace English words with Chinese words. Otherwise, you will be speaking Mandarin Chinese to Americans. Most Americans do not understand Mandarin Chinese.

原则 1

不要用汉字替代英文单词。否则，你跟美国人讲的是中文，不是英文。
而大部分美国人都不懂中文。

Most Chinese speak Mandarin Chinese, and many Chinese would like to learn to speak American English. The common thinking is to find a link between these two languages. What we tend to do is translate English words into Chinese: "Since I know how to speak Mandarin Chinese, if I am not familiar with an English word, I will find an equivalent Chinese word to use in place of the English word I am trying to learn. I will say Chinese words that *sound like* English." This is usually way off. It may sound fine to other Chinese, but in my experience, when I try speaking these words to Americans, they are lost.

中国人想学习美式英文，一个普遍的思维是找出两种语言之间的联系。我们往往会把英文单词翻译成中文："因为我知道怎么讲中文，所以如果我对一个英文单词不熟悉，我就会把我要学的那个英文单词替换成对应的中文。我会讲听上去像英文的中文"。也许其他中国人觉得没问题，但是以我个人经验来说，当我试着跟美国人说这些中文词的时候，他们一头雾水。

When I was in fifth grade back in Taiwan, my neighbor Micky, who is five years older than I am, showed me an English dictionary. Every English word in the dictionary had a Chinese equivalent sounding word or words. Well, I thought, it is not that hard to learn to speak

English. All I need to do is memorize the equivalent Chinese words and just use them. That is the origin of Chinese English speaking. You think you are speaking English, but you are actually speaking Mandarin Chinese. Most Americans do not understand Mandarin Chinese.

当我还在台湾读小学五年级的时候，我的邻居 Micky 比我大五岁，他给我看了一本英文字典，字典中的每一个英文单词后面都有对应的中文字或者中文词。我想，学讲英语也没那么难嘛。我要做的就只是记住那些对应的中文词，然后使用它们就好了。这就是中式英文口语的起源。你觉得你在讲英文，但实际上你在讲中文。

The Chinese and English languages are very different. The table below summarizes the major differences between these two languages.

中文和英文是非常不同的。下表总结了这两种语言主要的差别。

2 Very Different Languages
2种非常不同的语言

American English and Mandarin Chinese
英文(美式)和中文(普通话)

	American English 英文(美式)	**Mandarin Chinese** 中文(普通话)
Basic letters/sounds 字母/基本发音	26 letters of the English alphabet (A-Z) "英文字母表"里的26个字母 (A-Z)	37 basic sounds for Zhu-yin 37个基本发音（注音） Many more for Pin-yin 拼音的数量就更多了
Words spoken 语言特色	Long and expressive 长而富于表现力	Short and abrupt 简短
Choices of sounds/tones 发音/声调的选择	Many letters have multiple sound choices 许多字母有多种发音选择 There are at least 30 sound choices for all 5 vowels (A, E, I, O, U) 5个元音（A, E, I, O, U）至少有30种发音可选	A Mandarin Chinese character is sounded with a combination of 1 or 3 basic sounds 汉语的拼音都是通过1个或3个基本音组合在一起来发音的 Most Chinese characters have 4 tones to choose from 大部分汉字都有4种声调可选
Airy sounds 空气音	At least 25 airy sounds 至少有25个空气音	None of the 37 basic sounds (Zhu-Yin) are airy sounds 37个基本发音（注音）中，没有一个是空气音

66english.com

These essential differences between the two languages make English challenging for Chinese to pronounce and to speak—and vice versa.

两种语言间的这些本质区别，使英文发音和口语对中国人来说很有挑战性——反之亦然。

PRINCIPLE 2

No funny symbols; no more symbols like ʒ, ʊ, æ, ŋ, ʃ, θ, and so on.

原则 2

不再使用 ʒ, ʊ, æ, ŋ, ʃ, θ 等音标符号

In Taiwan, I started learning the English alphabet in the seventh grade. Every student had a big, thick English-to-Chinese dictionary. Every word in the dictionary had two short groups of funny symbols following it that represented the word's sounds. One symbol group matched the American pronunciation of the word and the other symbol group matched the British pronunciation. My teachers taught us the British version as the preferred pronunciation. Despite the dictionary my neighbor had shown me one or two years earlier, my teachers told me this was the new way to learn. I did not know any better. I adapted to the system, and I thought I did very well in my English classes.

在台湾，我从初一(7 年级) 的时候开始学习英文字母表。每个学生都有一本又大又厚的英汉字典。字典中的每个单词后面都有两组代表单词发音的音标符号。一组音标符号对应的是这个单词的美式发音，另外一组音标符号对应的是英式发音。我的老师教我们英式发音作为首选。

So there I was. I had two sets of symbols to learn, a British one and an American one. And it is much too confusing for most of us. To avoid confusion, the 66English Pronunciation Key System uses the existing twenty-six letters (A – Z), which you already know, to show pronunciation.

我得学习两种音标，英式的和美式的。为了避免混淆，溜溜英语体系抛弃了熟悉英式的和美式的音标，采用了现有的你更熟悉的 26 个字母 (A-Z) 以示发音。

For example, the word *base* is pronounced [bbb 'AAA' sss]. Repetition of the *B* and the *S* consonant sound reminds us to pronounce the sounds with a long, expressive tone. The repetition of 'AAA' means the sound is pronounced just like the first letter in the twenty-six letters: a long and expressive *A* sound. When I first started using the *A - Z* letters to show pronunciation, I showed students the pronunciation of the word *base* as [b 'A' s]. Students ended up pronouncing the word with short and abrupt sounds. However, once I started showing the pronunciation by using repeated letters, they start pronouncing the same word with longer tones. Then, the same word sounded more like American English.

比如单词 *base* 的发音是 [bbb 'AAA' sss]。重复多次的辅音 *B* 和 *S* 提醒我们，发一个长的，富于表现力的发音。重复的 '*AAA*' 意思是发音正如 26 个字母中的第一个字母一样：一个长的，富于表现力的 *A* 的音。当我首次使用字母 *A-Z* 来表示发音的时候，我用 [b '*A*' s] 给我的学生们展示了单词 *base* 的发音。学生们以短促的发音读出了这个单词。然而，当我开始使用重复的字母来表示发音的时候，他们就用长音读同样的一个单词。于是，这个单词听上去就更像美式英文了。

Footnote:

Many English words can sound slightly different due to regional accents. The pronunciation keys for words presented in this book are the sounds that I am aware of, the familiar sounds for Californians. If you live in the region (New York, Texas, etc.), go with the regional sound.

脚注:

许多英文单词的发音可能因为地区口语而有轻微的差别。本书中所展示的单词音标，是我所了解的，为加州人所熟知的发音。如果你住在纽约，德州等地，那就以当地的发音为准。

PRINCIPLE 3
The devil is in the tail[SM]
原则 3
魔音藏在尾巴里

You might have heard of the American expression, "The devil is in the details."

你也许听过一个美国习语 "魔鬼藏于细节里"

In my version of the phrase, "the devil is in the *tail[SM]*," we pay attention to the endings of English words. Many English words end with *D, M, P, S, T,* and so forth. If you are from the northern part of China, it is possible you will pronounce these ending letters by using an equivalent-sounding word in Chinese (*D* = 的, *M* = 母, *P* =普, *S* = 斯, *T* = 特). So, Las Vegas sounds like Las Vega 斯, thereby giving the word's tail end an added but incorrect emphasis.

我的版本是 "魔音藏在尾巴里"。多注意英文单词的结尾部分。许多英文单词都以 D, M, P, S, T 等等结尾。如果你来自中国北方，你有可能把这些单词的结尾字母用对应的中文汉字代替 (*D* = 的, *M* = 母, *P* =普, *S* = 斯, *T* = 特)。所以, *Las Vegas* 听上去像 "Las Vega 斯", 于是给单词的结尾加上了一个多余的但不正确的强调。

You will speak better English by changing the Chinese ending of the word 斯 to an English airy sound: S. *S* does not equal 斯. This is what I mean by "the devil is in the tail."

把单词结尾的汉字"斯"换成英文的空气音 *S,* 你的英文就能讲得更好。

If you are from the southern part of China, it is possible that you would totally ignore the ending letters because of one of the following reasons: 1) your English teachers did not teach you how to sound these ending letters; 2) you do not hear these ending letter sounds at all, so you do not pronounce them; 3) you arbitrarily think you do not need to pronounce the ending letters. So, *Las Vegas* sounds like *Las Vega* without the ending *S* sound.

如果你来自中国南方, 你有可能因为以下原因完全忽略单词结尾的字母: 1) 你的英语老师没有教你如何发结尾字母的音; 2) 你没有听到结尾的这些字母音, 所以你也不发它们的音; 3) 你以为结尾的字母并不需要发音。于是 *Las Vegas* 听上去就像不带结尾字母 *S* 发音的 *Las Vega*。

All you have to do is to pronounce the ending letter as the airy sound *S* and your English will sound more authentically American. This is why "the devil is in the tail."

你要做的就是发出结尾字母的空气音 *S,* 那么你的英语听上去就更像地道的美式英语。这就是我说"魔音藏于尾巴里"的意思。

In Chapter 6, I explain the importance of pronouncing the end letter sounds.

在第 6 章, 我会解释发出结尾字母的音的重要性。

PRINCIPLE 4
Exaggerate your pronunciation of English words
correctly, slowly and clearly.
原则 4
把英文单词的发音正确地，缓慢地，清晰地，夸张地说出来

To change from speaking short, abrupt Chinese words to long, expressive English words, we need to think differently and make sounds differently.

As mentioned in Principle 1, if we speak Chinese-equivalent words instead of English words, we will *automatically* speak English words in a short, abrupt manner.

从讲短促的中文词转变成讲长而富有表现力的英文词，我们需要转变思维。

正如原则 1 所提到的，如果我们说的是中文对应词，而不是英文单词，我们会不自觉的就把英文单词的发音读的很短促。

To make the dramatic change, we need to exaggerate our English pronunciation so that our mouth and tongue muscles get used to the new movements. Since this is a new process, slow down and start pronouncing words slowly. Once your muscles are used to these movements, you will move these muscles unconsciously. Over time, your speed will increase and you may achieve fluency.

要有这么巨大的转变，我们需要把我们的英文发音夸张化。这样，我们的嘴巴和舌头的肌肉才会习惯新的动作。由于这是一个新的学习过程，放慢速度，开始学着慢慢的发单词的音。一旦你的肌肉习惯了这些动作，你就会不知不觉地运动

到这些肌肉。久而久之，你的速度会得到提高，你也会变得更流利。

PRINCIPLE 5
Listen to and observe differences between sounds.
原则 5
"听"并"观察"发音之间的区别

As I mentioned when describing the six senses of the 66English System, we use our ears (Sense 4) to listen to the subtle differences between sounds that most people ignore.

正如我在描述溜溜英语体系中的"六官"时所提到的，我们用耳朵去听发音之间的细微差别，这些差别是大部分人会忽略的。

We use our eyes (Sense 5) to watch mouth shapes and tongue movements. If you can mimic the same mouth shapes and tongue movements, you can produce the same or very similar sounds. Using different mouth shapes and tongue movements will definitely produce different sounds.

我们用眼睛（第五官）去观察讲话人的口型和舌头的运动。如果你能模仿同样的口型和舌头运动，你就可能发出一个完全一样或者非常相似的音。使用不同的口型和舌头运动一定会产生不同的发音。

PRINCIPLE 6
Living in an environment—The affects of living in
a specific environment on language-developing skills.
原则 6
生活环境——生活在特定的环境中对语言技能的影响

If we speak, listen to, read, and write Chinese 100% of the time, or most of the time, then we are living in a Chinese-dominant environment whether we physically live in China or in the U.S. The 66English System can help you speak better American English—maybe even much better English than you ever expected. However, if you spend minimal time on speaking, listening to, reading, writing, or watching English-related materials, then your progress will be limited and you might not be able to move yourself up to the next stage. (The 8 stages of Speaking English. See Chapter 3.)

如果我们用 100% 的时间，或者大部分时间说，听，读，和写中文，那么不管我们住在中国还是住在美国，我们都生活在一个以中文为主导的环境中。如果你只花极少时间在说，听，读，写，或者看英文相关的材料上，那么你的进步会非常有限，不容易使自己进入下一个讲英语阶段。(讲英语的 8 个阶段，请见第 3 章。)

Have you had this kind of an experience? You are not sure about the pronunciation of a word, so you check your online dictionary, read the funny symbols, and are still confused. Then you ask a Chinese friend, who tells you a different answer. Where do you go from there? Either you pronounce the word the way you think it should be pronounced, or you just put it aside and forget about it.

你曾有过这种经历吗？有一个单词的发音你不确定怎么读，于是你查了在线词典，读了音标，之后仍然很迷惑。于是你询问一位中国朋友，他告诉你一个不同的答案。谁是对的？我们该何去何从呢？要么按照自己认为的方式发音，要么就把它放在一边 算了不理。

Here is my experience. When I was in high school, I watched a popular American TV show about puppets called *Thunderbirds*. It had something to do with the word *super*. One day, I was debating with a friend of mine about the pronunciation of *super*. I told my friend that according to the dictionary's funny symbols, it should sound like *siew-per*. My friend's girlfriend, who was studying at the American School in Taipei, happened to be around. She joined the conversation and said the word should be pronounced *suuu perrr*. I trusted my dictionary, rather than her. However, after I came to the U.S., I realized she had been correct. I started pronouncing *super* [*suuu perrr*] the way she did. In hindsight, I realized her English-learning environment was very different than mine.

在台湾念高中的时候，我每礼拜必看一部很红的木偶的美国电视剧 "雷鸟神机队"。它的剧情和单词 *"super"* 有点关系。有一天，我在和我的一位朋友争论 *"super"* 的发音。我告诉我的朋友，根据字典里的音标，它应该读 *siew-per*。我朋友的女朋友，她在台北的美国学校上学，当时正巧也在。她加入了我们的对话，说这个单词应该读 *suuu perrr*。我相信了我的字典，而不是她。但是，在我来到美国以后，我意识到，她是对的。我开始按照她发音的方式读 super [*suuu perrr*]。事后，我意识到她的英文学习环境跟我的差太多了。

Are you aware of the environment that you are in?

You might be living in an environment in which you do not have opportunities to speak English or have your English corrected by someone; you might not have opportunities to learn about or experience American culture.

你自己处在什么样的环境中吗？也许你生活在一个没有机会讲英文，或者没有人帮你纠正英文的环境里；你也许没有机会学习或者亲身体验美国文化。

It is my desire to use the help of technological advances to create such an environment. After my students learn the basics of English pronunciation, we advance to our online classes (which use video and audio), in which the students are speaking English 90% or more of time. Slowly, the students become comfortable speaking English in the sessions most of the time. They no longer make memorized speeches or read prepared scripts; instead, the students are experiencing real English conversations in the class. I receive comments like this: "In the beginning, I felt awkward about speaking and listening to English outside of a classroom setting. After a while, I got used to it, and I liked it. I never had an environment where I could talk with my friends in English and have someone correct my English as I was speaking…" Join us, you can live in the environment. Find out more at our website: www.66English.com.

我非常渴望能够利用科技的帮助来创造一个这样的环境。我住在 L.A., 有些学生住在 Dallas, 上海, 我们在网络上上课 (使用视频和音频)。刚开始, 大部分上课以中文为主。学生们学过英语发音的基础后, 更进一步, 英语的部分也越来越多, 也鼓励学生开始讲英文。慢慢的, 学生们适应在课程中大部分时间听讲英文。有些班 90% 甚至更多的时间学生都在说英文。他们不再说一些死记硬背的句子, 也不再去读事先写好的稿子; 学生们在课堂中进行了真正的英文对话。我曾收到这样的评论: "一开始, 我觉得在课堂环境讲英文和听英文都很吃力。过了一段时间之后, 我习惯了, 我喜欢这样! 从来没有过这样的环境, 能让我跟我的同学朋友讲英文, 还有人会纠正我讲的英文…"。 "溜溜英语体系" 可以帮助你讲更好的美式英文——也许是远远高于你的期望值的英文。有兴趣吗? 详情请见网站: www.66English.com。

Do the six senses and six principles sound and make sense to you? If yes, you might ask the following question:

如果懂了六感和六原则, 你也许会有以下疑问:

**Is there a shortcut I can take to improve my
English pronunciation right away?**

有没有捷径能让我马上提高我的英语发音呢?

Yes, there is a shortcut. You can improve your English pronunciation *immediately* simply by adjusting to a new way of thinking. See Chapter 7 for details.

有捷径。你只要调整思维方式, 能马上提高你的英语发音水平。详情请见第 7 章。

**Is there a shortcut I can take to learn
how to speak English in a more American style?**

有没有捷径能让我学会如何讲出更加美式的英文呢?

Yes. Start exaggerating your English pronunciation so that your mouth and tongue muscles get used to English's long, expressive muscle and tongue movements (Principle 4).

有捷径。开始把你的英文发音夸张化, 那么你的嘴巴和舌头的肌肉就会习惯英文的长而富有表现力的肌肉和舌头运动 (原则 4)。

Which sounds should I start learning first?
Which sounds will make the biggest impact on my English
speaking so that Americans can understand me better?

我该首先学习哪个发音呢?
哪些发音最能影响我的英文口语, 而让美国人能更好的理解
我呢?

The sounds that make the biggest impact are the A, E, I, O and U vowel sounds, as I mentioned in the Introduction. See Chapters 9 (I, O sounds) and 10 (A, E and U sounds) for details.

最有影响力的发音是: A, E, I, O 和 U 这些元音发音, 正如我在引言中所提到的。详情请见第 9 章 (I 和 O 的发音) 和第 10 章 (A, E 和 U 的发音)。

No matter what, English is the language for business throughout the world. Speaking English is a skill that can be learned and developed. I have done it, and I can help you reach your desired level.

无论怎样, 英文都是全世界通用的商业语言。讲英语是一门可学习可发展的技能。我做到了, 我也可以帮你大大提高你的水平。

CHAPTER 6

第六章

Getting Rid of Chinese English Accents Within Three Minutes, Guaranteed!

三分钟内，教你如何摆脱一些中式英语的口音。保证即刻见效！

Pronounce English Words Better than 90% of Native Chinese Speakers Who Live in the U.S.

你许多英语单词发音会比 90% 住在美国的中国人好！

How can I make such a bold guarantee as the one described in this chapter's title? I can make it because most people ignore some basic facts.

我怎么会做出如此大胆的保证呢? 因为大多数人都忽略了一些基本事实。

Let us have some fun with English words first:

Without referring to your iPhone, smartphone, iPad, PC or Mac, can you say which of the following is the correct spelling for an international icon?

我们先来玩个单词游戏:

没有你的 iPhone, 智能手机或 iPad 的帮助之下, 你认为下面哪个是这个国际性标志 (麦当劳) 的正确拼法呢?

McDonald
McDonalds
McDonald's

Next, how do you pronounce it?

接下来, 怎么发这个音呢?

麥当勞 (中文发音)

Mai don lau
Mai don nou
Mai don noud
Mai don nous
Mic don ald zzz

90% of native Chinese speakers do not add the *S* sound to the end of the word. If you do say the *S* sound in *McDonald's*, you are in the top 10%.

McDonald's is the correct spelling.

90% 的中国人都不发结尾的 's' 音。如果你在读 McDonald's 的时候发了 's' 这个音, 你就是前 10%! McDonald'**s** 是正确的拼法。

Try another example. We all know this famous place in southern California. How do you pronounce *Hollywood*?

我们都知道，南加州有个很有名的地方叫 'Hollywood'，怎么读这个地名呢?

好萊塢 or 荷裡活 or How Lai Wu?

90% of native Chinese speakers do not add the *D* sound to the end of the word *Hollywood*. If you do, you are in the top 10%. *Hollywood* is the correct pronunciation.

90% 的中国人都不发结尾的 'd' 这个音。如果你在读 'Hollywood' 的时候发了 'd' 这个音，那么你就是前 10%! 'Hollywood' 才是正确的发音。

Try some of these other examples, which prove people do not say the ending letters most of the time:

下面有一些其他例子，来证明结尾的字母常常被我们忽略而不发音。

Fren fry vs. *French fries*.

Unite State vs. *The United States* (People miss the *The* most of the time).

Unite Airline, UA, or '美联航' vs. *United Airlines*.

That's it. Why is this a big deal? We do not pronounce the ending letters (*D, K, P, S, T,* and *Z,* etc.) of numerous English words. You will take a big step toward losing your Chinese English accent simply by saying the ending letters correctly. Americans do not know how to say the word *Hollywood* without making the *D* sound or say the word *McDonald's* without making the *S* sound.

结尾字母不发音或者用中文词来发音，有什么大不了吗？沒什么大不了。中式英语口音而已。

简单地通过正确的发结尾字母的音，你就在摆脱中式英语口音上有了很大的进步。有许多单词我们都会忽略它的结尾字母 (比如 D，K，P，S，T，Z 等等)。因为美国人不知道如果不发 'd' 这个音，那么怎么说 'Hollywood' 这个字，也不知道如果不发 's' 这个音，怎么说 'McDonald's' 这个字。

Three minutes are up!

三分钟到了!

CHAPTER 7

第七章

The Devil Is in the Tail^{SM}

尾巴上的魔音

The Most Common Ones
最通用的一些字母:
D, K, P, S, T, and Z

Do these sound the same to you?

这些发音一样吗?

Good, goo

Food, fu

Peek, pee

Keep, key

Sense, sen

Peace, pea

Cute, Q

By the time you are done with this chapter, you will have learned the differences between these words, which is a huge return for a minimum investment on your part.

读完本章内容后，你就知道这些单词的区别。对你来说，小投资赢得大回报。

D, K, P, S, T, and Z are all airy (voiceless) sounds. In other words, you can pronounce them by pushing the air out of your mouth without making a sound. Many English words end with these letters, and this chapter summarizes these sounds.

字母 D, K, P, S, T and Z 都有空气音 (不发出声)。换言之，你可以通过把空气呼出嘴巴而不发出声音的方式来发这些音。许多英文单词都以这些字母结尾，本章是对这些字母发音的总结。

Here's the easy part in another free short lesson. You can learn to pronounce new sounds (D, K, P, S, and T) correctly in two minutes or less. Many Chinese pronounce these English letters by using Chinese sounds instead. So, for example, D sounds like 的 and P sounds like 普.

你可以在两分钟甚至更短的时间内. 学会这些新的字母音 (D, K, P, S 和 T) 的正确发音。有些中国人用中文的发音发这些英文字母的音。举例来说，D 的发音就像 "的"，P 的发音就像 "普"。

How can you differentiate between the English letter D and the Chinese 的 sound? Follow the steps described below.

1. Use one hand to touch your throat area and make the 的 sound. Can you feel the vibration of your throat?
2. Now, try to make the D sound. You should not feel any vibration when touching your throat.
3. Now try to pronounce the K, P, S, and T sounds without vibrating your throat. No vibrations? Great!

You have just learned to pronounce these sounds in two minutes or less.

怎样区分英文字母 *D* 和汉字 "的" 的音呢?

1. 用一隻手触摸喉部,并发出 "的" 的音。你能感觉到喉咙的震动吗?

2. 现在,试着发一个 *D* 的音。当你触摸喉部的时候,你不应该感受到任何喉咙的震动。

3. 现在,试着不让喉咙震动来发 *K, P, S* 和 *T* 的音。没有震动? 太棒了!

两分钟到了。

D

---

feed: without the *D*, Americans might think you are saying *fee* or *feet*.

单词 'feed'。如果不发 'd' 的音, 美国人可能会以为你说的是单词 'fee' 或者 'feet'。

food: without the *D*, Americans might think you are saying *fool*.

单词 'food'。如果不发 'd' 的音, 美国人可能会以为你说的是单词 'fool'。

need: without the *D*, Americans might think you are saying *knee or niece.*

单词 'need'。如果不发 'd' 的音, 美国人可能会以为你说的是单词 'knee' 或者 'niece'。

K
---

ask: without the K, Americans might think you are saying ass, a word that could be easily misunderstood.

单词 'ask'。如果不发 'k' 的音，美国人可能会以为你说的是单词 'ass'，一个很容易让美国人误解的单词。

back: without the *K*, Americans might think you are saying *bad*, *bed*, *bag*, *beg*, or *bat*.

单词 'back'。如果不发 'k' 的音，美国人可能会以为你说的是单词 'bad', 'bed', 'bag', 'beg', 或者 'bat'。

black: without the *K*, Americans might think you are saying *blog*, *block*, *bank*, or *bang*.

单词 'black'。如果不发 'k' 的音，美国人可能会以为你说的是单词 'blog', 'block', 'bank' 或者 'bang'。

check: without the *K*, Americans might think you are saying *chat*, *chic*, or *cheek*.

单词 'check'。如果不发 'k' 的音，美国人可能会以为你说的是单词 'chat', 'chic', 'cheek', 'chess', 'chest' 或者 'Chuck'。

P
---

map: without the *P*, Americans might think you are saying *mat*, *mad*, or *met*.

单词 'map'。如果不发 'p' 的音，美国人可能会以为你说的是单词 'mat', 'mad' 或者 'met'。

chip: without the *P*, Americans might think you are saying *cheap*, *cheat*, or *cheek*.

单词 'chip'。如果不发 'p' 的音，美国人可能会以为你说的是单词 'cheap', 'cheat' 或者 'cheek'。

laptop: without the *P*, Americans might think you are saying *letter* or *latter*.

单词 'laptop'。如果不发结尾 'p' 的音，美国人可能会以为你说的是单词 'letter', 'later' 或者 'latter'。

S and Z

S is the most missed-out sound. So many words end with *S*, and there are also the singular and plural expression differences between Chinese and American languages to take into account.

For example, *make sense* becomes *may sen*. There is no *K* sound in *make*; no *S* sound in *sense*.

's' 是最容易被忽略的音。许多单词都以 's' 结尾，而且中文和美语间的单数和复数表现形式上有着很大的差别。词组 'make sense' 听上去像 'may sen'。在 'make' 里没有 'k' 的音，在 'sense' 里也没有 's' 的音。

I wrote a note that ended, "*Thanks*, Ken Ma." One of my students asked me, "How come you have to add *S* after *thank*? Can I use *thank*?" When we see *S*, we think about the difference of singular versus plural. Do not try to analyze whether there should be an *S* or no *S*. Just say *thanks*. There is no need to choose between thank or thank*s*. It is *thanks*.

有写 emails 通常以 "Thanks, Ken Ma" 结尾。有个学生问我: "为什么你在 'thank' 后面加个 's' 呢? 我可以用 'thank' 吗?" 因为当我们看到 's' 结尾时, 我们会想单复数的问题, 去分析到底有 's' 还是没 's'。不要去选择到底是 'thank' 还是 'thanks'。就是 'Thanks'。

Another common problem is this: "Do I say *congratulation* or *congratulations*?" Many Chinese will write or say *congratulation*. Just use *congratulations*.

另一个很普遍的问题是: 我到底该说 'Congratulation' 还是 'Congratulations'? 许多中国人都会写或说 'Congratulation'。就是 'Congratulations'。

A common ending phrase in e-mail is: "Let me know if you have any *question*" or "Let me know if you have any *questions*."

Which one is correct?

The second one with the S is correct: "Let me know if you have any *questions*." I have seen many e-mails using the first version of the phrase (*question* without the *S*).

一个很普遍的邮件结束语:

"Let me know if you have any question." 或者 "Let me know if you have any questions." (如有问题请告知)。哪个才是正确的? 第二个有 's' 结尾的才是正确的。我看到好多中国人写的 emails 都用了第一个形式 (question 没有加 S)。

'*z*' has an interesting sound; many Chinese feel that '*z*' is a challenging sound.

'z' 的发音很有趣。很多中国人都觉得 'z' 是个很有挑战性的
发音。

Here are examples of the *z* letter making a *z* sound:

amaze [a **'mAAA'** zzz]

crazy [kkk **'rAAA'** 'zEEE']

dozen [**d^** z^nnn]

freeze [fff **'rEEE'** zzz]

jazz [ja zzz]

pizza [**'pEEE'** tzzz^]

zoo [zuuu]

zero [**'zEEE'** 'rOOO']

How should you pronounce the S letter with a Z sound? (Normally,
this happens at the end of a word.) Many students have asked me the
same question: when should they pronounce *S* or *Z*? To me, it is less
critical to pronounce *S* or *Z* than it is just to pronounce that part of
the word.

很多学生都问我 结尾的 's' 何时发 's' 音，何时发 'z' 音呢?
对我来说，发出这个音比 发 's' 音或者 'z' 音更重要。

I really do not have rules. As long as Americans understand exactly
what I am saying without having to make guesses, then my language
skills are working.

不管是发 's' 还是 'z' 的音，我自己没有规则可循。只要美
国人不用猜测就能正确的理解我说的英语及可。

According to this very loose, general rule, pronounce *S* at the end of
words that end with *K, P, Gh,* and *Th.*

如果一定要有个原则，那 当 's' 和结尾是 'k', 'p', 'gh' 和
'th' 这些字母在一起时, 's' 发 's' 的音。

bank => *banks* [sss]

suck => *sucks* [sss]

tank => *tanks* [sss]

chip => *chips* [sss]

cup => *cups* [sss]

tip => *tips* [sss]

high => *highs* [sss]

laugh => *laughs* [sss]

sigh => *sighs* [sss]

thigh => *thighs* [sss]

bath => *baths* [sss]

path => *paths* [sss]

myth => *myths* [sss]

For the rest, pronounce Z at the end:

其他情况下, 's' 在结尾发 'z' 的音:

boy => *boys* [zzz]

eye => *eyes* [zzz]

girl => *girls* [zzz]

new => *news* [zzz]

pea => *peas* [zzz]

scissor => *scissors* [zzz]

tie => *ties* [zzz]

T

---

bat: without the *T*, Americans might think you are saying *bad, bed,* or *bath.*

单词 'bat'。如果不发 't' 的音，美国人可能会以为你说的是单词 'bad', 'bed' 或者 'bath'。

bait: without the *T*, Americans might think you are saying *bay* or *base.*

单词 'bait'。如果不发 't' 的音，美国人可能会以为你说的是单词 'bay' 或者 'base'。

hot: without the T, Americans might think you are saying hug, hut, or hat.

单词 'hot'。如果不发 't' 的音，美国人可能会以为你说的是单词 'hug', 'hut' 或者 'hat'。

sit: without the *T*, Americans might think you are saying *sea, she, seat,* or *set.*

单词 'sit'。如果不发 't' 的音，美国人可能会以为你说的是单词 'sea', 'she', 'seat' 或者 'set'。

Let us review the questions from the beginning of this chapter. Do the following words sound the same?

我们再来回顾一下本章一开始的问题，他们读起来一样吗？

good ≠ goo
good [guuu ddd]

food ≠ fu
*foo_d_* [fuuu ddd]

peek ≠ pee
*pee_k_* ['PPP' kkk]; pee ['PPP']

keep ≠ key
*kee_p_* [kkk 'EEE' ppp]; *key* [kkk 'EEE']

sense ≠ sen
*sen_se_* [sss ennn sss]

peace ≠ pea
*pea_ce_* ['PPP' sss]; *pea* ['PPP']

cute ≠ Q
*cu_te_* ['QQQ' ttt]; *Q* ['QQQ']

No. They do not sound the same.

不，他们的发音不一样。

Whether American or Chinese, we all love pizza (≠ pee sa 批萨), especially if we are college or graduate students. It is convenient, hot, and tasty; what's not to like? We have learned the Z sound; how about the ZZ sound? Remember, *pizza* is spelled with ZZ. The *zza* is not sa, nor is it the American pronunciation of the Italian word *pizza* ['**pEEE**' tzzz ^].

不管是美国人还是中国人，我们都喜欢批萨，尤其是大学生和研究生。既便捷，又鲜辣可口，不是吗？

Pizza ≠ pee sa 批萨。 我们学了 'z' 的发音, 那 'zz' 的发音呢? Pizza 这个单词的拼写中有 'zz'。对于美国人来说,这个意大利单词 'pizza' 的发音中的 'zza' 不发 sa.

[ˈpEEEˈtzzz ^]

CHAPTER 8

第八章

The Most Useful Phrases in Spoken English

英文口语中最有用的单词

Pick Your American First Name

你的名字对于美国人来说, 容易发音吗?

Th sound

*Th*的发音

Do these sound the same?

这些单词听上去一样吗?

this, lease
thank you, Sun Q, 桑 *Q*
three, tree
tooth, tu s
teeth, tea s

faith, face
bathe, bass

By the end of this chapter, you should be able to understand the difference between these words. With some practice, you will be able to say the *Th* sound with ease.

到本章结尾时，你应该会知道这些单词之间的区别了。通过一些练习，你会很轻松地发 *Th* 的音。

In an American business environment, these four words or short phrases are used mostly in spoken and written communication:

在美国商业环境里，下面这四个单词/短语在交流的时候最常用，无论是在口语中还是写作中：

[The person's name] [对方的名字]
"Thank you." "谢谢"
"Please." "请"
"May I ....?" "我可以…吗?"

We should all learn to speak certain English words correctly right away. The expression foreigners in any country use the most is "thank you." In Spanish, the expression is *gracias*; in Chinese, it is 谢谢. We all learn those words.

一些英文单词可以马上现学现用。最常用的就是"谢谢"。

Thank you, Sun Q, 桑 Q.

However, we have a problem. The problem is the *Th* sound. That is not one of the 37 sounds found in Chinese, and it is not even in the English alphabet's twenty-six letters. Besides, it is an airy sound.

但是我们有一个问题, *Th* 的发音问题, 因为它不是中文里的 37 个发音之一。而且它也不在英文的 26 个字母表里! 此外, 它还带有空气音 (不发出声音)。

Here is how to pronounce the *Th* sound: stick your tongue out as far as possible (Principle 4: exaggerate pronunciation) and blow the air out while the tongue is out (see www.66English.com for a detailed video demonstration). You might feel awkward, embarrassed, or stupid sticking your tongue out, so you might retreat your tongue right away. Then the *Th* sound really does not come out. Once you have learned how to pronounce the *Th* sound, then you will find it easy to say words beginning with *Th* sounds (like *the*, *this*, and *that*) and words ending with *Th* sounds (*teeth*, *tooth*, and *faith*).

如何发 *Th* 的音? 把舌头伸出来, 越長越好 (原则 4, 夸张发音), 嘴巴闭起來, 把空气从牙齿和舌头的缝隙中吐出来, 这樣子, *Th* 的音就发出来了。 也许你觉得把舌头伸出来很为难/尴尬/愚蠢, 大多数人会马上把舌头收回去, 于是 *Th* 的音并没有完全的发出来。一旦你学会了如何发 *Th* 的音, 以 *Th* 音节开头比如 "the", "this", "that" 等等, 和以 *Th* 音结尾比如 "teeth", "tooth", "faith" 等等的单词就会很容易的发出来了。

Thank you [thhh annn 'QQQ']

Thank you for trying.

"Please."

"请"

Start with the word *ease* ['EEE' zzz].

You will end up with *please* [ppp '**lEEE**' zzz].

先从这些单词 ease 开始，再唸 please。

The *P* sound is an airy sound, so *P* ≠ 普.

P 的发音带有空气音, P ≠ 普。

"May I …?"

"我可以…吗?"

Using this phrase is a polite way to begin questions.

"*May I* have your e-mail address?"

"我可以知道你的邮箱地址吗?", 这是一种很礼貌的提问方式。

A person's name

对方的名字

Picture yourself in a crowd. If someone yells your name, it is possible you will drop whatever you are doing and start looking for the person yelling your name. Your brain is in tune to your own name.

想象你自己在人群中, 如果有人喊出你的名字, 不管你当时在做什么, 你都很有可能放下手头的事情然后开始寻找谁在叫你的名字。

There are many names, including English male and female names, and Chinese male and female names. Pronouncing these names can be challenging.

无论男性英文名，女性英文名，男性中文名或女性中文名，有
许多的名字的发音相当有挑战性。

Pronouncing a person's first name correctly becomes important,
too. If your Chinese first name is easy to pronounce and remember,
such as *Yo-yo* or *May-ling*, then keep your Chinese first name. If not,
pick an American name that is easy for both Americans and Chinese
to pronounce. Many Americans do not know how to pronounce
Chinese names like *Fei, Ng, Qi, Ue, Xi, Xu*, and so on.

把一个人的名字正确的读出来非常重要。如果你的中文名对
美国人来说既好读又好记，比如 *Yo-yo, May-ling* 等等，那么就
用你这个中文名。如果不是，那么建议就选一个对双方，不
管是美国人还是中国人，都很好发音的英文名。大部分美国
人都不知道如何读一些中文名，比如 *Fei, Ng, Qi, Ue, Xi, Xu*
等等。

**Some challenging common English male first names
to pronounce:**
一些不容易发对音的英文名 (男性):

David (David ≠ 大為; David ≠ 大衛; David ≠ Day Vee)
Because of the *V, I,* and the *D* at the end.
因为 "V"，"I" 和结尾的 "D" 的发音。

Bill (Bill ≠ 必有)
Because of the *I* and *L* sounds.
因为 "I" 和 "L" 的发音。

Charlie (Charlie ≠ 掐你; Charlie ≠ 查理)
Because of the *Ch* and *R* sounds.
因为 "Ch" 和 "R" 的发音。

Jim (Jim ≠ 近; Jim ≠ 近母)
Because of the *J*, *I*, and *M*. The name *Jim* started my English pronunciation journey forty years ago.
因为 "J", "I" 和 "M" 的发音。40 年前，英文名 "Jim" 让我开始了我重新学习英文发音之路。

John (John ≠ 醬; John ≠ 约翰)
Because of the *J* sound and the *N* sound at the end. *John* is challenging. It took me almost twenty years after coming to the U.S. to say the name *John* correctly.
因为 "J" 和结尾 "N" 的发音。John 这个名字非常有挑战性，我花了差不多 20 年 (在我来到美国之后) 才把 John 这个名字读对。

Michael (Michael ≠ 麥可; Michael ≠ 麥克)
Because of the ending *L* sound.
因为结尾 "AEL" 的发音。

Paul (Paul ≠ 砲; Paul ≠ 保罗)
Because of the ending *L* sound.
因为结尾 "L" 的发音。

Philip (Philip ≠菲力甫)
Because of the *I*, *L*, and *P* sounds.
因为 "I", "L" 和结尾 "P" 的发音。

Richard (Richard ≠理查)
Because of the *I*, *Ch*, *R*, and the *D* at the end.

因为 "I", "Ch", "R" 和结尾 "D" 的发音。

William (William ≠ 威廉)
Because of the *I*, *L*, and *M* sounds.
因为 "I", "L" 和结尾 "M" 的发音。

Some challenging common English female first names to pronounce:
一些不容易发对音的英文名 (女性):

Linda (Linda ≠ 琳達)
Because of the *I* and *N* sounds.
因为 "I" 和 "N" 的发音。

Barbara (Barbara ≠ 芭芭拉)
Because of the *R* sound.
因为 "R" 的发音。

Jessica (Jessica ≠ 潔西卡)
Because of the *I* sound.
因为 "S", "I" 的发音。

Nancy (Nancy ≠ 莳西)
Because of the second *N* sound and the *C* sound.
因为第二个 "N" 和 "C" 的发音。

Mary (Mary ≠ 玛莉)
Because of the *A* and the *R* sounds.
因为 "A" 和 "R" 的发音。

Ruth (Ruth ≠ 璐司)

Because of the *R* and *Th* sounds.

因为 "R" 和 "Th" 的发音。

If one of the names mentioned above is your English first name, keep it. It is your name, so pronounce it correctly.

如果你的英文名字正好是上面提过的英文名之一，请继续用这个英文名。既然这是你选的名字，那广至少把它讲对。

Below are some suggested, common names that are easy for Chinese to pronounce correctly. (I purposely avoid the names with challenging sounds and with ending *N* and *L* sounds.)

以下的建议都是对于中国人来说很容易发音的名字（我避免选用一些带有挑战性的 "I", "L" 的发音，和以 "N" 结尾发音的名字)。

Suggested English male first names:

男性英文名建议:

Andy [**annn** 'DDD']

Barry [**bbb a** 'rEEE']

Bob [bahhh bbb]

Ed [eddd]

Fred [fff reddd]

Harry [**hhh a** 'rEEE']

Jesse [**jjj e** 'CCC']

Jerry [**jjj e** 'rEEE']

Joe [jjj 'OOO']

Larry [**le** 'rEEE']

Mike ['mIII' kkk]

(Mike is a nickname for Michael) (Mike 是 Michael 的简称)

Peter [**'PPP'** terrr]

Tony [**'tOOO'** 'nEEE']

Suggested English female first names:

女性英文名建议:

Amanda [^ **man** d^]

Amy [**'AAA'** 'mEEE']

Angela [**an** j^ l^]

Anna [**an** n^]

Betty [**bbb e** 'TTT']

Debra [**de** br^]

Donna [**dawwwn** nahhh]

Lisa [**'lEEE'** s ^]

Lucy [**luuu** 'CCC']

Maria [m^ **'rEEE'** ^]

May [m 'AAA']

Tina [**'TTT'** n^]

Here is an example of a short conversation that uses all four of the most commonly used words or short phrases (a person's name, "please," "thank you," and "may I...?"):

一个用到所有 4 个最常用单词和短语 (人名, "请", "谢谢", "我可以...吗)"? 的小对话:

You: "David, may I contact you by e-mail?"

你: "David, 我可以用邮件跟你联系吗?"

David: "Sure, please do."

David: "当然可以。"

You: "May I have your e-mail address?"

你: "我可以知道你的邮箱地址吗?"

David: "Yes, it is dave… @qq.com."

David: "好的。邮箱是 dave…@qq.com。"

You: "Thank you, David."

你: "谢谢你, David。"

Back to the question I asked in the beginning of the chapter, do these words sound the same?

再次回到本章伊始的问题, 这些单词听上去一样吗?

these ≠ Lease

these ['thEEE' zzz]

lease ['lEEE' sss]

Thank you ≠ Sun Q ≠ 桑 Q

Thank you [thhh **ann** 'QQQ']

three ≠ *tree*

three [thhh 'rEEE']

tree [ttt 'rEEE']

too<u>th</u> ≠ *tu* S

too<u>th</u> [tuuu thhh]

tee<u>th</u> ≠ tea S

tee<u>th</u> ['TTT' thhh]

fai<u>th</u> ≠ face

fai<u>th</u> ['fAAA' thhh]

face ['fAAA' sss]

ba<u>the</u> ≠ bass

ba<u>the</u> ['bAAA' thhh]

bass ['bAAA' sss] (a musical instrument) (低音)

bass [bbb a sss] (a kind of fish) (鲈鱼)

No. They do not sound the same.

不，他们发音是不一样的。

CHAPTER 9

第九章

The Confusion Starts Here

混淆始于此

I and O sounds

I 和 O 的音

The *I* sound

I 的音

Do these words sound the same?

这些单词的发音听上去一样吗?

b<u>i</u>t, *beat*

d<u>i</u>p, *deep*

f<u>i</u>t, *feet*

<u>i</u>ll, *eel*

<u>i</u>t, *eat*

<u>i</u>tch, *each*

lip, leap

sh_*t, sheet

While I am not advocating the use of the word *sh*t*, I know it is often used—it is almost an everyday word. If you are going to say it, say it correctly!

虽然我不提倡说 "sh*t" 这个单词，但是我知道它很常用——它几乎成了日常用语。如果你一定要说这个词，至少把它说对！

There are at least five sounds for the *I* sound, as described in the following sections.

I 至少有 5 种发音，如下所述。

The mysterious *I* sound: The *'E'+ye* sound
神秘的 *I: 'E'+ye*

I mentioned this sound in Chapter 2, so I will not repeat it here.

这个发音在第二章曾提过，所以此处不再重复。

You should be able to determine the differences between the following:

你应该会区分以下单词发音的不同：

Bit [bbb 'E'+ye ttt] sounds very different than *beat* ['BBB' ttt].

Bit [bbb 'E'+ye ttt] 和 *beat* ['BBB' ttt] 的发音有很大的差别。

Fit [fff 'E'+ye ttt] sounds very different than *feet* [fff 'EEE' ttt].

Fit [fff 'E'+ye ttt] 和 *feet* [fff 'EEE' ttt] 的发音有很大的差别。

Some of my students could say these words correctly after one session. We were all impressed with ourselves. I hope you can also achieve this within a short period of time, too. At the very least, you should be able to hear the difference between these words.

我的一些学生，通过一节课的学习之后都能正确的发这些单词的音。我们都为自己感到骄傲。我希望你也能在短时间内实现这个目标。至少，你应该能"听"出这些单词的区别。

When I am working with students, we start with *it* and go on to *bit*. They get it. Then, in the next session I will say, "Okay, let's try *milk*." When students combine the *I* and *L* together, they lose the *I* sound, and the word becomes *milk* ['mEEE' lll kkk]. *L* is hard on its own, and the *IL* combination is particularly challenging. The word *ill* ['E'+ye lll] becomes *eel* ['EEE' lll]. *Bill* [bbb 'E'+ye lll], either the male's name or the invoice, sounds like *bee-*有['BBB' lll].

在教学生的时候，我们从 *it* 发音开始，然后到 *bit* 发音。他们做到了。接下来，下节课我会说，"好，我们来试试看 *milk* 的发音"。 当学生们把 *I* 和 *L* 组合在一起的时候，他们会把 *I* 的音丢了，单词就变成了 *mee-lk* ['mEEE' lll kkk]。*L* 本身发音就很难，*IL* 的组合就难上加难了。单词 *ill* ['E'+ye lll] 就变成了 *eel* ['EEE' lll]。*Bill* [bbb 'E'+ye lll], 不管是男性名字还是发票的意思，听上去都像 *bee-* 有 ['BBB' lll]。

The long *I* sound
长音 *I*

The long *I* sound is an easy one for native Chinese speakers. It sounds just like the letter *I* in the English alphabet. Think of *I'm*, *IBM*, *iPad*, *iPhone*, *iTunes*, *ice*, *idea*, *icon*, *item*, and so forth.

长音 *I* 对于中国人来说很简单，它听上去就和英文字母表中的字母 *I* 一样。诸如 *I'm, IBM, iPad, iPhone, iTunes, ice, idea, icon, item* 等等。

IBM ['III' 'BBB' 'MMM']

ice ['III' sss]

idea ['III' '**DDD**' ^]

I'm ['III' mmm]

iPad ['**III**' ppp a ddd]

iPhone ['**III**' 'fOOO' nnn]

The third *I* sound
第三种 *I* 的发音

This version sounds like the letter *E*, as in *chief*.

这个 I 的发音，听上去就像字母 *E*，比如单词 *chief*。

chief [chhh 'EEE' fff]

The fourth *I* sound
第四种 *I* 的发音

In this version, the *I* sound is silent.

这个 *I* 不发音。

The word *again* has two pronunciations. In one, the *I* is silent: *again* [^ **ggg** e nnn]. With the alternate (and less popular) pronunciation, *again* is pronounced with the *E* sound [^ 'gAAA' 'E' nnn].

单词 *again* 有两种发音。第一种 *I* 不发音: *again* [^ ggg e nnn] 。另外一种发音 (不那么常用), *again* 发 *E* 的音 [^ 'gAAA' 'E' nnn] 。

The last *I* sound
第五种 *I* 的发音

---

just a short i sound

短的 i 音

mini [mi 'nEEE']

To return to the question posed at the beginning of this chapter, do these words sound the same?

回到本章伊始的问题, 这些单词的发音一样吗?

bit ≠ *beat*

dip ≠ *deep*

fit ≠ *feet*

ill ≠ *eel*

it ≠ *eat*

itch ≠ *each*

lip ≠ *leap*

sh*t ≠ *sheet*

bit [bb 'E'+ye ttt]; *beat* ['BBB' ttt]

dip ['DDD' 'E'+ye ppp]; *deep* ['DDD' ppp]

fit [fff 'E'+ye ttt]; *feet* [fff 'EEE' ttt]

ill ['E'+ye lll]; *eel* ['EEE' lll]

it ['E'+ye ttt]; *eat* ['EEE' ttt]

itch ['E'+ye chhh]; *each* ['EEE' chhh]

lip [lll 'E'+ye ppp]; *leap* ['lEEE' ppp]

sh*t [shhh 'E'+ye ttt]; *sheet* [shhh 'EEE' ttt]

No. They do not.

不, 他们不一样。

The *O* sound
O 的发音

There are at least six ways to pronounce the letter *O* in a word.

单词里面的字母 *O*, 至少有 6 种不同的发音。

The long *O* sound
长音 *O*

This sound is pronounced just like the letter *O* in the English alphabet.

这个发音和英文字母表中的字母 *O* 一样。

c<u>o</u>ke ['**kOOO**' kkk]

d<u>o</u>se ['**dOOO**' sss]

l<u>o</u>w ['l**OOO**']

<u>o</u>at ['**OOO**' ttt]

tomat<u>o</u> [t^ '**mAAA**' 't**OOO**'] (The last *O* in the word.)

(单词里的最后一个 *O*)

zer<u>o</u> ['**zEEE**' 'r**OOO**']

The second *O* sound
第二种 *O* 的发音

This sound is pronounced just like *ahhh*. To make this sound, open your mouth in a big, round shape just like the shape of the *O* letter (Principle 4: make big, exaggerated mouth movements). We advocate making big mouth and long tongue movements in our methods of teaching. Once you get used to the muscle movements, your mouth will not need to open that widely and your tongue will not need to stick out that much, but the sounds will still be there.

这个发音就像 *ahhh*。把嘴巴张开，形成一个大的圆形发这个音，就像字母 *O* 的形状一样（原则 4：做出大的，夸张的嘴巴运动）。我们的教学方法提倡做出大嘴巴和长舌头的动作。一旦你习惯了肌肉的动作，你的嘴巴就不需要再张那么大，舌头也不需要伸那么长了，但是你的发音已经对了。

Bob [bahhh bbb]

box [b**ahhh** kkk sss]

copy [k**ahhh** 'PPP']

fox [fahhh kkk sss]

Here is a word that has two *O* sounds: *Apollo* [ahhh **pahhh** 'lOOO']. The first *O* sounds like *ahhh*, while the second *O* sounds like the letter *O*.

Apollo 单词含有两种 *O* 的发音: *Apollo* [ahhh **pahhh** 'lOOO'] 。第一个 *O* 的发音就像 *ahhh*, 第二个 *O* 的发音就像字母 *O* 一样。

The third *O* sound
第三种 *O* 的发音

This is pronounced like the *awww* sound. You know how to pronounce the word *saw*. Take out the *S* sound, and the *awww* you are left with is how the third *O* should sound.

这个发音像 awww。你会发单词 saw (锯子，see 的过去式)
的音，把 S 去掉，剩下的 awww 就是第三种 O 的发音。

Donna is a Chinese friend of mine. We met in L.A. when I was
attending graduate school at the University of Southern California.
Later on, she got married and moved back to Taiwan. We met again
when I was visiting Taiwan a few years later. She told me she was
donut. I was confused. She said people in Taiwan called her by her
English first name, *Donna*, but the sounds they used sounded like
donut.

Donna 是我的中国人朋友。我们是在洛杉矶认识的，那时我
在南加大读研究生。之后，她结婚并搬回了台湾。几年后我
回台湾，我们又见面了。她告诉我她是 *donut* (甜甜圈)。我
很迷惑。她说，许多在台湾的朋友都叫她的英文名 *Donna*，
但是他们的发音很像 *donut*。

If your English first name is *Donna* and you pronounce your name
dou-na, when you introduce yourself to an American, you sound like
you are saying "I am *Donut*." What is in an American's mind when
she hears "I am *Donut*"? The American thinks, "I hear *Donut*. Did I
hear right? Let me ask again…"

如果你的英文名是 Donna，你把它发成 dou-na，当你向美国
人介绍自己的时候，你听上去就像在说: "I am donut"，如果这
个美国人听到 "I am donut"，她会怎么想呢?她会想: "我听到
donut，我听错了么? 我再问一遍吧…"。

This book's cover illustrates the misunderstandings that can arise
from the wrong *O* sound choice.

本书封面展示了由于 *O* 的发音选择错误而造成的误解。

Donna [**dawwwn** nahhh] vs. *donut* [**'dOOO'** n^ ttt].

Just by reading the pronunciation, you can tell they sound very different.

通过比较单词后面的溜溜音标, 你应该能分辨出这两个发音的显然不同。

boss [bawww sss]

sorry [**sawww** 'rEEE']

The fourth *O* sound
第四种 *O* 的发音

This should be pronounced with a very short ^ sound. Since I have not found a better way to show how to pronounce this specific sound, I use a carat symbol, ^, to express the sound. The sound of '^' is very short and abrupt.

这个发音是一个很短的 ^ 音。由于尚未找到更好的方式来代表这个特别的发音，我借用了符号 "^" 来表示这个音。"^" 这个音很短促。

Monday [**m^n** 'dAAA'] (Many Chinese pronounce this word 忙 day.)
(许多中国人都会把这个单词读作 "忙 day")。

monkey [**m^n** 'kEEE']

love [**l^** vvv]

potato [p^ '**tAAA**' 'tOOO'] (The first *O* in the word.)
(单词中的第一个 *O*)

son = *sun* [s^ nnn]

tomato [t^ '**mAAA**' 'tOOO'] (The first *O* in the word.)
(单词中的第一个 *O*)

The fifth *O* sound
第五种 *O* 的发音

This pronunciation uses a short *U* sound.

这种发音，是一个短音 *U*。

woman [**www u** mmm ^ nnn]

The last *O* sound
最后一种 *O* 的发音

In this pronunciation, the *O* is silent.

这种 *O* 是不发音的。

phoenix [fff **'EEE'** nnn i kkk sss]

CHAPTER 10

第十章

The Confusion Compounds
混上加混

The Rest of the Vowels: *A*, *E*, and *U*
剩下的元音: *A, E*和*U*

Do these words sound the same?

这些单词的发音听上去一样吗?

bad, bed

tape, tap, tab, Ted

matrix, mattress, match, Mitch, much, March

June, Joan

paper, pepper

sax, sex, six, seeks, socks, sucks

The *A* sound
A 的发音

There are at least eight ways to pronounce an *A* sound in a word.

单词里的 *A* 至少有 8 种发音。

The first *A* sound
第一种 *A* 的发音

This is pronounced like the letter *A*.

这种发音就和字母 *A* 一样。

*a*pe ['AAA' ppp]

c*a*pe [kkk 'AAA' ppp]

t*a*pe [ttt 'AAA' ppp]

M*a*cy's [**'mAAA'** 'CCC' sss]

p*a*in ['pAAA' nnn]

p*a*int ['pAAAn' ttt]

p*a*ste [**'pAAA'** sss ttt]

s*a*fe ['sAAA' fff] (Check out how to pronounce *F* in Chapter 12.)

(如何发 *F* 的音，请见第 12 章)

s*a*ve ['sAAA' vvv] (Check out on how to pronounce *V* in Chapter 12.)

(如何发 *V* 的音，请见第 12 章)

vacation ['vAAA' **'kAAA'** shhh ^ nnn] *A* is used twice in the word *vacation*. In both instances, the pronunciation sounds like the letter *A*.

在单词 *vacation* 中, *A* 出现了两次。两种情况下, 它都发字母 *A* 的音。

To pronounce the word *matrix*, start with *-ick* ['E'+ye kkk].

Then add *trick* [trr 'E'+ye kkk]. Then *tricks* [trr 'E'+ye kkk sss].

Then *matrix* [**'mAAA'** trr 'E'+ye kkk sss].

Pronounce the words slowly, clearly, and correctly (Principle 4).

想要发单词 *matrix* 的音, 从 *-ick* ['E'+ye kkk] 开始, 然后发 *trick* [trr 'E'+ye kkk] 的音, 再发 *tricks* [trr 'E'+ye kkk sss] 的音, 最后就发出了*matrix* [**'mAAA'** trr 'E'+ye kkk sss] 的音, 单词的发音要缓慢, 清晰, 正确 (原则 4)。

The second *A* sound
第二种 *A* 的发音

This is pronounced like a short *a* sound. Words such as *have, had, hat, bad, dad, mattress, match,* and *master* all fall into this category. This short *a* sound gets easily confused with the short *e* sound (*bad* vs. *bed*, for example).

这种发音是一个短音 *a*。比如单词 *have, had, hat, bad, dad, mattress, match,* 和 *master* 都属于这一类。短音 *a* 很容易和短音 *E* 弄混 (比如 *bad* 和 *bed*)。

To make the *a* sound, open your mouth big and make a short *a* sound.

想要发出短音 A, 张大嘴巴, 发一个短促的 a 音。

ha̲ve [hhh a vvv]

ha̲d [hhh a ddd]

Ha̲rry [hhh **a** 'rEEE']; *Harry* ≠ 哈利

ha̲t [hhh a ttt]

da̲d [ddd a ddd]

ma̲ster [**mmm a** sss ttt errr] (This is not pronounced [**mmm ahhh** sss ttt errr]; the latter is a British pronunciation.)

(不读 [**mmm ahhh** sss ttt errr]，后者是英式发音。)

The third *A* sound
第三种 *A* 的发音

This is pronounced like the *ahhh* sound.

这种发音是发一个 *ahhh* 的音。

a̲rt [ahhh 'RRR' ttt] (See Chapter 11 for the R sound.)

(R 的发音请见第 11 章)

ba̲r [bahhh 'RRR']

fa̲r [fahhh 'RRR']

fa̲ther [**fff ahhh** thhh ^ rrr]

ha̲rd [hahhh 'RRR' ddd]

wa̲ffle [**wahhh** fff lll]

The fourth *A* sound
第四种 *A* 的发音

This is pronounced like *awww*.

这种发音是发一个 *awww* 的音。

d<u>au</u>ghter [**dawww** ttt errr]

f<u>a</u>ll [fawww lll]

s<u>aw</u> [sawww]

s<u>au</u>ce [sawww sss]

The fifth *A* sound
第五种 *A* 的发音

This is pronounced like a short *e* sound.

这种发音就像一个短音 *e*。

ag<u>ai</u>n [^ **ggg e nnn**]

ban<u>a</u>na [b^ **ne** n^] *(banana ≠ 爸辣辣; banana ≠ 把那那)*

B<u>a</u>n<u>a</u>n<u>a</u> [b^ **ne** n^]. There are three *A* sounds separated by two *N* sounds. The first and the third *A* sound the same, while the middle *A* sounds different. Why? I do not know. That is how Americans say the word. If you say *banana* the Chinese way [ba na na], will Americans understand you? Probably. However, it is not that hard to pronounce *banana* the way Americans pronounce it. Take baby steps for a while, and then look back. You will notice how much you have improved.

Banana [b^ **ne** n^]。三个 *A* 的音被两个 *N* 的音隔开。第一个和第三个 *A* 的发音是一样的。但是中间的 *A* 发音却不同。为什么? 我不知道。美国人就是那么说的。如果 *banana* 读成 [ba na na],美国人会理解你吗? 也许吧。但是,想以美国人的方式发 banana 的音并不难。慢慢一步一步来,然后往回看。你会发现你有了多大的进步!

The sixth *A* sound

第六种 *A* 的发音

This is pronounced like a short *I* sound.

这种发音是一个短音 *I*。

orange [awww r i n jjj]

The seventh *A* sound

第七种 *A* 的发音

This is pronounced like ^.

这种发音就像 ^。

banana [b^ **ne** n^]

career [k^ '**rEEE**' rrr]

China [chhh '**III**' n^]

Korea [kaw '**rEEE**' ^]

The last *A* sound

最后一种 *A* 的发音

This *A* sound is silent.

A 不发音。

pea ['PPP']

each ['EEE' chhh]

The *E* Sound

E 的发音

There are at least five ways to pronounce the *E* sound, including a long *E* and a short *E* sound.

E 的发音至少有五种，包括长音 *E* 和短音 *E*。

The long *E* sound

长音 *E*

This sounds like the letter *E.*

这个发音和字母 *E* 的发音一样。

be [b 'EEE']

e-mail ['EEE' **'mAAA'** lll]

he [hhh 'EEE']

she [shhh 'EEE']

we ['wEEE']

weed ['wEEE' ddd]

Many long *E* sounds come with the *EA* or *EE* combination.

许多长音 *E* 都是 *EA* 或 *EE* 的字母组合。

beach ['BBB' chhh]

beat ['BBB' ttt]

each ['EEE' chhh]

ear ['EEE' rrr]

teach ['TTT' chhh]

bee ['BBB']

beet ['BBB' ttt]

deed ['dEEE' ddd]

fee ['fEEE']

feed ['fEEE' ddd]

feet ['fEEE' ttt]

pee ['pEEE']

peep ['pEEE' ppp]

The short *E* sound

短音 *E*

---

bed [bbb e ddd]

beg [bbb e ggg]

best [bbb e sss ttt]

edit [**e** d i ttt]

The Fed. [fff e ddd] (The United States Federal Reserve System)
(美联储)

get [ggg e ttt]

let [le ttt]

Ted [ttt e ddd]

red [rrre ddd]

How should we differentiate between
the short A and the short E sound?
我们应该如何区别短音 *A* 和短音 *E* 呢?

First, we need to know (by using the brain, Sense 1) that they sound different yet very similar. We native Chinese speakers often *assume* they sound the same. If I am not careful about pronouncing some words, sometimes I confuse myself, as well as other Americans.

首先, 我们得知道 (用大脑, 第一官) 它们听上去很像但不同。许多中国人常以为它们的发音是一样的。如果我自己没用心的去发一些单词 *(A, E)* 的音, 有时我自己都搞糊涂了, 也有可能美国人听不懂我讲的是哪个字。

Look at these words. Do they sound the same?

请看这些单词。它们的发音一样吗?

Fall, fell, feel

Sale, seal, steal, steel, stale

You should know by now that they do not sound the same.

现在你应该知道，它们的发音并不一样。

Second, train your ears (Sense 4) to listen to the subtle differences. This can be particularly hard if our ears cannot naturally hear the differences.

其次，训练你的耳朵 (第四官) 去听出一些细微的差别。

Third, learn to pronounce these sounds correctly (using the mouth and the tongue, Senses 2 and 3) and to watch (using the eyes, Sense 5) the mouth shape when others pronounce these sounds. I will use gestures (hand gestures, Sense 6) to exaggerate the pronunciation.

再次，学习正确的发这些音 (用嘴巴和舌头，第二官和第三官)，在别人发这些音的时候，学着去看他的嘴型。**嘴型不对，发音一定不对。**

The third *E* sound
第三种 *E* 的发音

This sounds like the mysterious *i* sound or the *'E'+ye* sound.

这种发音就像神秘的*I*的发音或者说发 *'E'+ye* 的音。

interest [**'E'+ye nn** ter ris ttt]

The fourth *E* sound
第四种 *E* 的发音

This sounds like the letter *A*.

这种发音和字母 *A* 的发音一样。

b<u>e</u>ta [bbb **'AAA'** t^]

The last *E* sound
最后一种 *E* 的发音

The *E* is silent.

这个 *E* 不发音。

ap<u>e</u> ['AAA' ppp]

Skyp<u>e</u> [sss 'kIII' ppp] (*Skype* does not sound like *sky-pee* [sss 'kIII' 'PPP'].)

(Skype 不读 sky-pee [sss 'kIII' 'PPP'].)

The *U* sound
(*U* ≠ 幼)

The *U* sound. That is an easy one; there is an equivalent sound in Chinese. 幼, right? Not exactly.

U 的发音。这个很简单; 有一个与之对应的中文发音, 幼, 对吗? 并非如此。

Here is the difference between the Chinese 幼 and the English *U*. Look at the mouth shape of these two sounds (use your eyes and your ears). In the Chinese 幼, the mouth rarely moves. In the English *U*, the lips and the mouth really move forward, making the so-called fish mouth (魚嘴巴). This mouth shape also demonstrates more muscle movements for American English.

中文的幼和英文的 *U* 的差别在于这两个发音的嘴型 (用你的眼睛和耳朵)。中文的幼, 嘴巴几乎不动。英文的 *U,* 嘴唇和嘴巴要往前伸, 做出一个所谓的鱼嘴巴。这个嘴型也表现出, 美式英文有着更多的肌肉运动。

There are at least six ways to make the *U* sound.

U 的发音至少有 6 种。

The long *U* sound

长音 *U*

This sounds like the letter *U*.

这个发音就是字母 *U* 的发音。

fuse ['fUUU' zzz]

refuse ['rEEE' **'fUUU'** zzz]

abuse [^ **'bUUU'** zzz]

juice ['jUUU' sss]

unit ['**UUU**' nnn i ttt];

unite ['UUU' '**nIII**' ttt]

united ['UUU' '**nIII**' ti ddd]

you ['UUU']

The second *U* sound
第二种 *U* 的发音

This is the short ^ sound.

这种发音是一个短音 ^ 。

bus [b^ sss]

but [b^ ttt]

cut [kkk ^ ttt]

dusk [d^ sss kkk]

dust [d^ sss ttt]

desk [ddd e sss kkk]

disk [ddd 'E'+ye sss kkk]

hut [h^ ttt]

nut [n^ ttt]

peanut ['**pEEE**' n^ ttt] (peanut ≠ 匹那)

sun [sss ^ nnn]

The third *U* sound
第三种 *U* 的发音

This is the short *u* sound.

这种发音是一个短音 *u*。

*bl**u**e* [bbb luuu]

*fr**u**it* [fff ruuu ttt]

*t**u**be* [tuuu bbb]

The fourth *U* sound
第四种 *U* 的发音

This is the *e* sound.

这种发音是发 *e* 的音。

*yog**u**rt* [**'EEE' 'OOO'** gerrr ttt]

The fifth *U* sound
第五种 *U* 的发音

This is the short *i* sound.

这是一个短音 *i*。

*min**u**te* [mi ni ttt]

The sixth *U* sound
第六种 *U* 的发音

This is the silent *u* sound.

这个 *u* 不发音。

laugh [lll aaa fff]

guitar [gi **'tRRR'**]

Let us review the question from the beginning of the chapter. Do these words sound the same?

让我们来回顾一下本章伊始的问题。这些单词的发音一样吗?

bad ≠ *bed*

tape ≠ *tap* ≠ *tab* ≠ *Ted*

matrix ≠ *mattress* ≠ *match* ≠ *Mitch* ≠ *much* ≠ *March*

June ≠ *Joan*

paper ≠ *pepper*

sax ≠ *sex* ≠ *six* ≠ *seeks* ≠ *socks* ≠ *sucks*

bad [bbb a ddd]

bed [bbb e ddd]

tape ['tAAA' ppp]

tap [ttt a ppp]

tab [ttt a bbb]

Ted [ttt e ddd]

ape ['AAA' ppp]

mattress [**mmm** a tr e sss]

match [**mmm a** chhh] (The *T* is silent.)

Mitch [**mmm 'E'+ye** chhh] (The *T* is silent.)

much [**m^** chhh]

March [**mmm arrr** chhh]

June ['jUUU' nnn]

Joan ['jOOO' nnn]

CHAPTER 11

第十一章

The Challenging Sounds
最具挑战性的字母

L, *R*, and *N*

Do these sound the same?

这些单词的发音听上去一样吗?

load, road, node

lead, read, need

light, right, night

led, red, net

If you watch American football games, you might have heard of the name "NFL" (National Football League). The *L* is at the end. Many native Chinese speakers cannot differentiate among these *L*, *R*, and *N* sounds. These are the most difficult sounds for native Chinese speakers to master. If I have done a good job teaching you, you will be able to differentiate among these three sounds. With practice, you will be able to say the above words correctly.

如果你平时看美国橄榄球比赛，你应该听说过 NFL (美国橄榄球联盟)。字母 L 在结尾处。许许多多的中国人都发不清这个 L 的音。对于中国人来说，L 是相当难掌握的字母发音。如果我教的对，你将学会区分这三个字母 (L, R and N) 的发音。通过练习，你会正确的把以上这几个字母的音发出来。从我开始学 ABC 的 30 年之后，才学会 L 的正确发音。你不需要花 30 年来学这些发音，但是，是要花点时间。

To my best estimate, 99% of native-speaking Chinese pronounce the letter *N* incorrectly. Well, to many native Chinese people's surprise, the English letter *N* is not pronounced like the Chinese 恩. If you can learn to pronounce the letter *L* correctly, then pronouncing the letter *N* is not that difficult to master.

据我估计，99% 的中国人的字母 *N* 的发音都不正确。大多数人发字母 *N* 的音很像 "恩"。如果你学会正确的发字母 *L* 的音，那么 *N* 就并没那么难掌握了。

The *L* Sound

I think *L* is the most difficult letter of the entire English alphabet for native Chinese to learn. When I was in Taiwan, we were taught to pronounce *L* like "e-漏," or "爱漏," which are easier for Chinese to pronounce. Again, in these cases we were pronouncing an English letter *L* with Mandarin Chinese sounds.

我认为在整个字母表中，*L* 对我们来说是最难学的。当我在台湾的时候，老师教我们*L*的发音类似 "e-漏"，"爱漏"。

Take the word *cool*, with the *L* at the end. "Coo 爱漏" is too much trouble to say. Just say "coo" or "ku." To complicate matters, the word 酷 and the sound of "coo"or "ku"are all so popular these days that they can be seen and heard everywhere.

单词 "cool" — L 在结尾，读 "coo 爱漏" 不顺。所以读 "coo" 或者 "ku"。中文的 "酷" 字最近也很流行，我们到处都能看到和听到。

I did not really learn the L sound until 1991. I didn't think I had a problem with it because no one really corrected my L sound. My parents moved to the U.S. in the early 80s. Then, in 1991, my father had a stroke. After the incident, he had to go through speech therapy and relearn how to speak. An American speech therapist was trying to teach English to a seventy-five-year-old Chinese man recovering from a stroke who barely spoke English in the first place. The therapy did not go very far. However, I got to know the speech therapist, who was a very nice woman. She said I had a problem with the letter L. I said, "Oh, really?" At that time, I had a French poodle. I did not say *poodle*, but I said *poodle* [pu 'dOOO'] 仆斗. I ended up spending an hour a week with the therapist for about two months. I paid her to correct some of my English mispronunciations, L among them. I finally learned to say *poodle* [puuu dlll], not *poodle* [pu 'dOOO'], and *people* ['PPP' plll], not *people* ['PPP' 'pOOO'].

直到 1991 年我才真正的开始学习L的发音。之前，我并不认为我的 L 发音有任何问题——没人来纠正过我的 L 发音。我的父母在 80 年代初期来到美国，1991 年，我的父亲患了中风。出院之后，医生采取语言复健治疗，重新学习说话。请语言矫正专家教他讲英语。一个美国语言矫正专家，试着教一位从中风恢复的，基本没讲过英语的 75 岁高龄的中国老人讲英语! 不用说，这肯定持续不了多久。然而，我逐渐认识了这位语言矫正专家 (抱歉，我不记得她的名字了)，一位非常友善的美国女士。她说我的字母 L 的发音有问题。

我说 "噢! 真的吗?" 之后的两个月, 我每周都花 1 个小时跟她在一起, 我付钱请她纠正我的一些英文发音—— L 是其中的一个。那时我养了一隻法国贵宾犬 "poodle" (在我们的网站上 www.66english.com 有我和 Minouche 的合影), 我把 "poodle" 唸成 仆斗 "pu-dOOO"。两个月之后, 我终于学会说 poodle [puuu dlll, not pu-'dOOO'], people ['PPP' plll, not 'PPP' 'pOOO'] 。

Here is how to pronounce the L sound:

1. Open the mouth.
2. Make a long 'e' sound.
3. Move the tongue up and touch the upper palate while continuing to make the long 'e' sound.
4. Continue opening the mouth and keep the mouth shape after the 'e' sound ends.

普通话的发音没有像这样的嘴巴和舌头的组合运动。如何发 L 的音?

1. 张开嘴巴。
2. 发一个长音 e。
3. 舌头向上伸, 触及上颚, 同时继续发长音 e。
4. 在 e 的音发完之后, 继续张开嘴巴, 保持嘴型。

Most of us either close or semi-close the mouth right after the tongue touches the palate; thus, the L sound really does not come out (Principle 4).

大多数人都会在舌头触及上颚之后, 马上闭上或者半闭上嘴巴, 于是 L 的发音没发出来。(原则 4, 夸张发音)。

Words that either start with L or have an L in the middle are easy to pronounce:

以 *L* 开始 或者 *L* 在中间的单词，比较容易发音:

eleven [e **le** vvv nnn]

lead ['lEEE' ddd]

led [le ddd]

light ['lIII' ttt]

load ['lOOO' ddd]

A word that ends with *L* is much harder to pronounce:
以 *L* 结尾的单词发音，对中国人来说相当难:

Bill [bbb 'E'+ye lll]

deal ['dEEE' lll]

eel ['EEE' lll]

fall [fawww lll]

feel ['fEEE' lll]

ill ['E'+ye lll]

kill [kkk 'E'+ye lll]

The *N* sound

During my high school years in Taiwan, I was playing guitar in a local amateur band and singing background vocals while preparing to get into college. My voice was not good enough as a lead singer, but I always wanted to improve my singing. After I came to the U.S., finished my graduate studies, and started working, I earned some money. I was single at that time and had no major expenses, so I started taking singing lessons. It was 1978, six years after I had started speaking English to Americans. The singing teacher told me my *N* sounded funny. My *N* sounded perfect to me, just like 恩. He showed me how to pronounce it correctly. At that time, I thought I copied the *N* sound pretty well. I really did not learn how to make the *N* sound correctly until I learned how to pronounce *L*. The ending of the *N* sound is so subtle that most Chinese cannot hear it, let alone copy it.

在台湾读高中时，我在一个当地的业余乐队中弹吉他及唱和声。我的声音不夠格担任主唱，但我总想让自己唱得更好。来到美国以后，读完了研究所，开始工作。那时我还是单身，没有大的开销 (没有女朋友)，我找美国老师教我唱歌。那时是 1978 年，是自从我开始跟美国人讲英语的 6 年之后。我的老师告诉我，我的字母 *N* 的发音很奇特。我认为自己的 *N* 的发音足够好了，*N* 就像 "恩"。他教我正确的发 *N* 的音，我认为我已经学会了 *N* 的发音。实际上直到我学会了发 *L* 的音之後，才知道如何正确的发 *N* 的音。*N* 结尾的发音是如此的细微，大多数人都听不到它，更不用说讲它了。

So, the word *in* is not the same as 印 and *on* is not the same as 昂.

所以，单词 "in" ≠ 印，单词 "on" ≠ 昂。

Here's how to make the *N* sound:

1. Open the mouth.
2. Make a long 'e' sound.
3. Move the tongue up and touch the upper palate while making the 'e' sound.
4. Continue opening the mouth and keep the mouth shape.
5. Before the *N* sound ends, open the jaw and drop the tongue. The mouth opens more widely, which is the very

subtle ending of the *N* sound. Most of us do not hear it at all.

如何发 *N* 的音?

1. 张开嘴巴
2. 发一个长音 e
3. 舌头向上伸, 触及上颚, 同时发 n 的音。
4. 嘴巴继续张开, 保持嘴形
5. 在 n 的音结束前, 张开下颌, 舌头放下来, 现在嘴巴张的更大了。这就是*N*的发音快结束时的极其细微的结尾音。大多数人听不到它。

As you can see, making the *N* sound involves several steps. Once you have learned the *L* sound, the *N* sound is actually pretty easy.

发 *N* 的音有 5 个步骤。一旦你学会了发 *L* 的音, *N* 的发音就非常的容易了。

*bon**d*** [b^ nnn ddd]

*i**n*** ['E'+ye nnn]

*li**ne*** ['lIII' nnn]; *lio**n*** ['lIII' ^nnn]

*o**n*** [awww nnn]

*onli**ne*** [awww nnn 'lIII' nnn]

The *R* sound

In Beijing, China, people like to end Chinese words with 兒. So, 花 sounds like 花兒, and 鸟 sounds like 鸟兒. 兒 sounds like the letter *R*, so Chinese just replace the letter *R* with 兒. Unfortunately, the two sounds are not the same. If you do this, you are pronouncing an English letter *R* with a Mandarin Chinese sound.

北方人会在汉字的结尾处加个 "兒"。所以，"花" 听上去是 "花兒"，"鸟" 听上去是 "鸟兒"。"兒" 听上去很像字母 *R*，于是我们直接把字母 *R* 用"兒" 替代。他们发的音并不一样。

R is a tongue twister. It is the second most difficult letter in the English alphabet for Chinese to pronounce. The speaker has to curl his or her tongue up in order to pronounce it. That is too much work for the Chinese, so many Chinese ignore the *R* sound in a word and simply do not say it. As a result, ba<u>r</u> sounds like ba, fa<u>r</u> sounds like fa, ca<u>r</u> sounds like ca, <u>r</u>ed sounds like led, and so on. To get rid of your Chinese English accent, make an effort to curl your tongue when there is an *R* letter in a word.

R 非常饶舌。对我来说，它是英文字母表中第二难发音的字母。为了发这个音，你必须把舌头卷上去，对中国人来说这太辛苦了，所以许多中国人不发单词中 *R* 的音。 如此，"bar" 听上去像 "ba"，"far" 听上去像 "fa"，"car" 听上去像 "ca"，"red" 听上去像 "le" 等等。想要摆脱中式英文口音，在单词中有字母 *R* 的时候，就把 *R* 的音發出來。

Making an *R* sound is a three-step process. What? A three-step process just for one sound? You must be kidding me! It is the truth. Moreover, I have seen huge success in students pronouncing the *R* sound with this three-step process I have developed.

Here is how to pronounce the *R* sound:

1. Open your mouth wide and make a very long *ahhh* sound.

2. While continuing to make the same *ahhh* sound, use your two hands (Sense 6) to push your cheeks in. Now, your

mouth looks like a fish mouth.

3. While still making the *ahhh* sound, curl your tongue up to the back of the upper palate. Now, the *R* sound comes out naturally.

如何发 *R* 的音:

1. 张大嘴巴, 发一个很长的 *ahhh* 的音,

2. 当你正持续发 *ahhh* 音的时候, 用你的双手 (你的双手, 六感中的第六感) 往里推你的双颊——你的嘴巴看起来像个鱼嘴巴,

3. 当你还在发 *ahhh* 音的时候, 把舌头往上颚的后方卷上去。*R* 的音自然而然的就发出来了。

By now, you should know *L*, *N*, and *R* sound very different. It takes four steps to make an *L* sound, five steps to make an *N* sound, and three steps to make an *R* sound.

现在你应该知道了 *L, N* 和 *R* 的发音有很大的区别: 发 *L* 的音有 4 个步骤, 发 *N* 的音有 5 个步骤, 发 *R* 的音有 3 个步骤。

Let us reference the question I posed in the beginning of the chapter. No, these words do not sound the same.

让我们重新回顾本章伊始的那个问题, 他们的发音不一样。

lead ≠ read ≠ need

led ≠ red ≠ net

light ≠ right ≠ night

load ≠ road ≠ node

lead (v.) ['lEEE' ddd] (meaning – to guide) (带领)

read ['rEEE' ddd] (Present tense. Not past tense)

(现在式，不是过去式)

need ['nEEE' ddd]

led [le ddd]

red [re ddd]

net [ne ttt]

light ['lIII' ttt]

right ['rIII' ttt]

night ['nIII' ttt]

load ['lOOO' ddd]

road ['rOOO' ddd]

node ['nOOO' ddd]

If you cannot say these words correctly, this question might come up again for you: "Why can't Americans understand me?" Americans cannot understand because they just do not know which word you were trying to say: *load, road,* or *node?*

如果以上的单词的发音你发不对，那么同样的问题又来了："为什么美国人听不懂我讲的英文？"很可能美国人就是不知道你到底在试着说哪个词—— *load? road? node?*

CHAPTER 12

第十二章

Letters Starting with a Sound H, M, Q, X, F, V, J, and G

The *H* sound

When I started learning the alphabet, I would say *H* as *e chhh* because that is how I was taught in Taiwan.

我刚开始学 ABC 的时候，我把 *H* 发成 "e chhh"，因为在台湾的时候老师就是这么教的。

Here is how to pronounce the letter *H* ['AAA' chhh]. It is simple.

如何发字母 *H* ['AAA' chhh] 的音？它很简单。

H in the word produces an airy sound:

H 在一个单词里，带有空气音：

hello [h^ 'lOOO'] (*Hello* ≠ 哈囉 (**ha** 囉))

hot [h ahhh ttt]

hut [h ^ ttt]

The *M* sound

(*M* ≠ 挨木; *M* ≠挨母)

M itself is very expressive. To pronounce the *M* sound, make an 'e' sound, then close the mouth with the *mmm* sound. Open the mouth after making the sound.

M 本身就很富于表现力。如何发 *M* 的音?

1. 发一个 "e" 的音,
2. 然后闭上嘴巴同时发 "*mmm*" 的音,
3. 发完这个音之后, 张开嘴巴。

Chinese from the northern part of China will emphasize the ending of *M* with a Chinese 母 sound, while Chinese from the southern part of China (Taiwan and Hong Kong included) will leave out the *M* sound; the *M* is truncated. "Some" sounds like "son", "di*me*" sounds like "dine", "ti*me*" sounds like "tine", and "mo*m*" sounds like "ma".

中国北方的口音, 会发出中文的 "母" 这个音来强调结尾的 *M;* 中国南方的口音会省略这个 *M* 的音。"Some" 听上去像 "son", "di*me*" 听上去像 "dine", "ti*me*" 听上去像 "tine", "mo*m*" 听上去像 "ma"。

*di*m* [ddd 'E'+ye mmm]

*di*me* ['dIII' mmm]

*Ji*m* [jjj 'E'+ye mmm]

*Ti*m* [ttt 'E'+ye mmm]

*ti*me* ['tIII' mmm]

*To*m* [ttt ahhh mmm]

Another common phrase that gets massacred: "*You're welcome.*" Chinese will say: "*U wel-con.*" We miss the *R* in the word *you're* and we miss the *M* sound at the end of the word *welcome.*

另一个常用语 "You are welcome." 常听到 "U wel-con"。 我们忽略了单词 "You're" 中的 *R* 的发音, 也忽略了单词 "welcome" 结尾处的 *M* 的发音。

The Q sound

The letter *Q* is very popular in Chinese publications and on ChineseTV these days. It is easy for Chinese to pronounce the letter *Q* and Chinese speak it frequently.

字母 *Q* 常出现在中国出版物和电视里, 口语里也常用。 对中国人来说 发字母 *Q* 的音很容易。

Most of the words with *Q* letters in them include the pairing *qu.*

大部分有字母 *Q* 的单词, 都带有字母组合 *qu*。

aqua [**ahhh** kwahhh]

equip [i **kw i** ppp]

frequent [**fff** '**rEEE**' kwennn ttt]

mosquito [m^ sss '**kEEE**' 'tOOO']

quad [kwahhh ddd]

quarter [kw **orrr** terrr]

query [**kwe** 'rEEE']

quiet ['**kwIII**' e ttt]

quit [kw 'E'+ye ttt]

quite ['kwIII' ttt]

question [**kwe** sss chhh ^^^ nnn]

queue ['QQQ']

quiz [kw 'E'+ye zzz]

squid [skw 'E'+ye ddd]

The *X* sound

(X ≠ 挨克死)

Most native Chinese speakers think *X* is easy to pronounce. However, what makes *X* challenging is that it is actually three distinct sounds—e kkk sss—compressed into just one letter. Normally, the *kkk* sound is missed altogether, and the *sss* is sometimes truncated. So, "e<u>x</u>cuse me" sounds like "e 死 Q 死 me," "bo<u>x</u>" sounds like "boss", "fo<u>x</u>" sounds like "foss", and "ta<u>x</u>i" sounds like "ta-see".

X 的发音好像很简单。使 *X* 变得很有挑战性的原因是——它有三个音节 "e kkk sss" ——同时存在于一个字母里。通常，"kkk" 的发音完全被忽略了，"sss" 的发音有时候也没了。所以，"e<u>x</u>cuse me" 听上去像 "一死 Q 死 me"，"bo<u>x</u>" 听上去像 "boss"，"fox" 听上去像 "foss"，"taxi" 听上去像 "ta-see"。

To make the sound of the letter *X*, make a 'e' sound, and follow it with *kkk* and *sss* sounds.

如何发字母 "X" 的音?

先发一个 e 的音，然后按顺序发 "kkk" 和 "sss" 的音。

When the letter *X* is in a word, the northern Chinese will pronounce all three sounds with equivalent volume, while the southern Chinese will ignore either the *kkk* or *sss* sounds.

当字母 *X* 藏在单词里的时候，中国北方的口音会发出三个音节 (挨克死)，中国南方的口音 会忽略 "kkk" 或者 "sss" 的发音。

e<u>xc</u>use [iks '**QQQ**' zzz]

e<u>x</u>ecute [**ek** '**CCC**' 'QQQ' ttt]

e<u>x</u>it [ek zi ttt]

fi<u>x</u> [fff 'E'+ye kkk sss]

ta<u>x</u>i [**ta** kkk 'CCC']

The *F* and *V* sounds

(F ≠ 挨付)

The pronunciation of *F* and *V* is similar, the upper teeth bite the lower lip to make both the *F* and the *V* sounds.

F 和 *V* 的发音很相似，上牙齿需要咬住下嘴唇才可以发出 *F* 和 *V* 的音。

To make a *F* sound, make an 'e' sound. When the upper teeth bite the lower lip, then you should make the *fff* sound.

如何发 *F* 的音?

发一个 e 的音，上牙齿咬住下嘴唇，然后发一个 "fff" 的音。

If the upper teeth do not bite the lower lip, then F sounds like 夫. The name *Frank*, for instance, sounds like *flank*, while *French* becomes *flen*.

如果上牙齿不咬住下嘴唇，那么 F 听上去就像"夫"。英文名"Frank"听上去就发成了"flank"。

beef ['BBB' fff]

face ['fAAA' sss]

faith ['fAAA' thhh]

fox [fahhh kkk sss]

leaf ['lEEE' fff]

To make a V sound: Use the upper teeth to bite the lower lip and make the *vvv* sound; after making the *vvv* sound, open the mouth to end the *V* sound.

如何发 V 的音?

上牙齿咬住下嘴唇，发一个"vvv"的音，发完"vvv"的音之后，张开嘴巴，结束 V 这个音。

If the upper teeth do not bite the lower lip, then the *V* sounds like the *W* sound. Thus, "thank you *very* much" (a common phrase for Chinese) sounds like "thank you *walley* much."

如果上牙齿不咬住下嘴唇，V 的音听上去就像"W"的音。那么"thank you very much"(对中国人来说的一个常用语) 听上去就像"thank you wa-lee much"。

Dave ['dAAA' vvv]

live (adj.) ['lIII' vvv]

live (v.) [lll 'E'+ye vvv]

save ['sAAA' vvv]

very [ve 'rEEE']

The _J_ and _G_ sounds

(_J_ ≠ 賊 and _G_ ≠ 雞)

For both _J_ and _G_, you need to curl your tongue to make the sound.

J 和 G 两个音，都需要卷舌，音才能发出。

To make a _J_ sound, make a _jjj_ sound by curling the tongue; then, make a _AAA_ sound.

如何发 J 的音?

卷舌，发一个 "jjj" 的音，然后发一个 "AAA" 的音。

Jack [ja kkk]

Jay ['jAAA']

James ['jAAA' mmm zzz]

Jim [jjj 'E'+ye mmm]

majesty [**mmm a** j^ sss 'TTT']

project [**pr^** je kkk ttt]

To make a _G_ sound, make a _jjj_ sound by curling the tongue; then, make a _EEE_ sound.

如何发 G 的音?

卷舌，发一个 "jjj" 的音，然后发一个 "EEE" 的音。

There are two ways to make a *G* sound in a word, as described below.
发单词中的 *G* 的音，有两种方式。

G with a *jjj* sound:
G 带有 "jjj" 的发音:

<u>G</u>eorge [jorrr jjj]
magic [**mmm a** j 'E'+ye kkk]

G with a *ggg* sound:
G 带有 "ggg" 的发音:

go ['gOOO']
leg [le ggg]

Now, how about when *G* is at the end of the word? After all, many words end with *-ing*, like *sing*, *singing*, and so on. Does the ending *G* have a sound or not? Most Chinese think there is no sound. However, there is a *ggg* sound in there. Since the *ggg* sound is very subtle, most Chinese do not hear it. When we say the word *sing*, it sounds like *sing* ['CCC' n] without the *G* sound. In *sing* ['CCC' ing], the *G* has a very subtle, airy sound.

那么当 *G* 在单词结尾的时候，还有当许多单词以 "ing" 结尾，比如 "<u>sing</u>", "<u>singing</u>" 等的时候， 情况又是怎么样的呢？ 结尾的 *G* 到底发不发音呢？大多数中国人认为不发音。但实际上. 有一个 "ggg" 的音存在。由于 "ggg" 的音非常细微，大部分中国人都听不到它。所以当我们说单词 "sing" 的时候， 它听上去像没有 "g" 音的 ['CCC' n]。Sing ['CCC' ing]。这个 "g" 带有非常细微的空气音。

CHAPTER 13

第十三章

The Remaining Tail Sounds B, C, W, Ch, Ph, and Sh

The *B* sound

B in a word is pronounced with an airy sound.

B 在单词中, 带有空气音。

Bob [bahhh bbb]

bass (a musical instrument) = *base* ['bAAA' sss]

boss [bawww sss]

bib [bbb 'E'+ye bbb]

Some final *B*s in words do not have any sounds, not even airy sounds. In these cases, the *B* is silent.

有些单词结尾的 *B* 并不发音, 连空气音也没有。*B* 是无声的。

bomb [bahhh mmm]

comb ['kOOO' mmm]

dum<u>b</u> [d^ mmm]

num<u>b</u> [n^ mmm]

The *W* sound

(*W* ≠ 達布溜)

I was taught to pronounce this letter *W* as 達布溜. I was surprised to learn that *W* means *U* plus *U*, so *W* is a double *U* ⌈ d ^ ɥlll 'ᴜᴜᴜ' ⌉.

在台湾，老师教我 *W* 的发音是 "達布溜"。

当我知道 *W* 意思是 U + U = W = double U [d ^ ɥlll 'UUU']
的时候，我太惊讶了。

W in a word produces an airy sound.

W 在单词里带有空气音。

<u>w</u>ait [wuu 'AAA' ttt]

<u>w</u>all [wuu ahhh lll]

<u>w</u>ar [wuu ahhh 'RRR']

<u>w</u>aste [wuu 'AAA' sss ttt]

<u>w</u>atch [wuu ahhh chhh]

<u>w</u>ay [wuu 'AAA']

The C sound

(C ≠ 西)

To pronounce the letter *C*, touch the top and bottom teeth together and make the airy sound *sss*. Then, make the *EEE* sound. So, you pronounce *C* [sss + 'EEE'].

如何发字母 *C* 的音?

上排牙齿和下排牙齿咬合在一起，发出一个空气音 "sss"，然后发一个 'EEE' 的音。所以, C = sss + 'EEE'。

If the letter *C* is in a word like the examples below, it sounds like the *kkk* sound.

字母 *C* 在单词中时, *C* 的发音像 "kkk"。

c̲at [k a ttt]

c̲ut [k^ ttt]

dis̲c̲ [d 'E'+ye sss kkk]

Eri̲c̲ [**e** r 'E'+ye kkk]

magi̲c̲ [**mmm a** j 'E'+ye kkk]

The *Ch* sound

There are at least three *Ch* sounds.

Ch 至少有 3 种发音。

The basic *Ch* sound:

最基本的 "chhh" 音：

bea<u>ch</u> ['bEEE' chhh]

<u>Ch</u>ina [chhh **'III'** n^]

<u>Ch</u>inese [chhh 'III' **'nEEE'** zzz]

<u>ch</u>urch [chhh **urrr** chhh]

ea<u>ch</u> ['EEE' chhh]

tea<u>ch</u> ['tEEE' chhh]

Ch can also sound like *kkk*:

Ch 听上去像 "kkk"：

<u>Ch</u>rist [kkk 'rIII' st]

<u>Ch</u>ristmas [kkk r'E'+ye s m^ sss]. The *T* is silent. 这个 T 不发音。

Ch can also sound like *shhh*:

Ch 听上去像 "shhh"：

<u>Ch</u>icago [shhh 'i' **kahhh** 'gOOO']

The *Gh* sound

There are at least three *Gh* sounds.

Gh 至少有 3 种的发音。

The basic *ggg* sound:

最基本的 "ggg" 音：

ghost [ggg 'OOO' sss ttt]

Gh can sound like *fff*:

Gh 听上去像 "fff":

enough ['E'+ye n ^ fff]

laugh [lll aaa fff]

The silent *Gh*:

Gh 不发音，*Gh* 是无声的:

high [hhh 'III']

though [thhh 'OOO']

The *Ph* sound

Ph can sound like *fff*:

Ph 听上去像 "fff":

graph [gra fff]

Joseph ['**jOOO**' s^ fff]

phase ['fAAA' zzz] (*face* ['fAAA' sss])

Philip [fff '**E'+ye** l 'E'+ye ppp]

phrase [frrr 'AAA' zzz]

The *Sh* sound

The basic *shhh* sound:

最基本的 "shhh" 音:

di__sh__ [ddd 'E'+ye shhh]

fi__sh__ [fff 'E'+ye shhh]

__sh__ake [shhh 'AAA' kkk]

__sh__eep [shhh 'EEE' ppp]

CHAPTER 14

第十四章

Now, the Numbers, Please

现在轮到数字了

Zelo, one, two, tree, fo, fi, si or *seeks, se* or *sewen, A, nigh, ten* (Chinese English)

vs.

Zero, one, two, three, four, five, six, seven, eight, nine, ten (American English)

We all deal with numbers, but 95% of native Chinese speakers do not pronounce *zero* through *ten* correctly.

我们都会和数字打交道——但是 95% 土生土长的中国人的 0 到 10 的发音是不正确的。

Why? The pronunciation is incorrect because four out of these eleven numbers contain the *N* sound (*one, seven, nine,* and *ten*). *N* is the most overlooked letter. Once you are able to pronounce the letter *L* correctly (as I discussed earlier, *L* is the most challenging letter for Chinese natives to pronounce), you can pronounce *N* easily. (See Chapter 11 for a guide to pronouncing *L, N,* and *R.*)

为什么呢? 因为在这 11 个数字里 (0 到 10), 有 4 个数字 (one, seven, nine and ten) 都带有 N 的发音。N 是 26 个字母 中最被忽略的字母。一旦你学会了正确的L发音 (L 是英文字 母里最难发音的一个字母), N 就很容易发音了。(L, R, N 的 发音请见第 11 章)。

Do these sound the same?

这些听上去一样吗?

one, won, own

three, tree

four, for, fork, fort

five, life

six, sax, sex, seeks, socks, sucks

eight, "A," aid

nine, line, lion, lie

You know by now that these words do not sound the same. After finishing this chapter, you should be able to hear the differences between them, at the very least. With practice, you should be able to say these numbers without confusing American listeners, who will know which numbers you are trying to say.

你应该知道, 它们的发音听上去并不一样。读完本章后, 你 应该至少能够 "听出" 这些不同。通过练习, 你应该能 "说 出" 这些数字, 而且美国人并不会搞错——他们知道你到底 在说哪些数字。

0 – Zero (zero ≠ ze lo)

zero [**'zEEE'** 'rOOO']

For some reason, very few native Chinese speakers say this number correctly.

很少的中国人能正确的发这个数字 0 的音。

1 – *one* [wuuu nnn] (*one* ≠ 万)

2 – *two* [tuuu]

3 – *three* (*three* ≠ *tree*)

If a native Chinese speaker does not know how to pronounce the *Th* sound, then *three* will sound like *tree*.

如果不会发 *Th* 的音, 那么 "three" 会听上去像 "tree"。
three [thhh 'rEEE']

4 – *four* [fff orrr]

5 – *five* ['fIII' vvv]

6 – *six* (*six* ≠ *sex, six* ≠ *seeks*)

Because of the confusion between the *I* and *E* vowel sounds, Chinese speaking English often—and wrongly—use these words interchangeably.

由于搞不清元音 *I* 和 *E* 的发音, 这些单词常被——错误地——互换使用。
six [sss 'E'+ye kkk sss]

7 – *seven* [**se** vvv nnn]

8 – *eight* ['AAA' ttt]

Often, Chinese incorrectly pronounce *eight* like the letter *A*, with no *T* at the end. That is how I used to say it too. When I said the number *eight*, I said "*A*." If I were describing a sequence of combined letters and numbers, the other party would not know if I was saying a letter or a number. That was my mistake. It took me a few years after I came to the U.S. to learn to say *eight*.

Eight 常被不正确的发成字母 *A* 的音——结尾没有 *T* 的音。我曾经就是这么读的。当我说数字 *eight* 的时候，我说 *A*。如果有一系列的字母和数字结合在一起，那么对方不知道我到底说的是字母 *A*，还是数字 *eight*。来美国之后，我花了好几年时间才学会说数字 *eight*。

9 – *nine* (nine ≠乃恩; nine ≠ line)

Because of the confusion between *N* and *L*, *nine* sounds like *line*. There is an equivalent sound in Chinese; thus, *nine* sounds like *nigh*.

由于搞不清 *N* 和 *L* 的发音，*nine* 听上去像 *line*。因为有对应的中文发音，所以 *nine* 听上去像 *nigh*。

nine ['nIII' nnn]

10 – *ten* [te nnn]

To get rid of your Chinese English accent when saying the numbers, learn the *N* sound.

学会发 *N* 的音，你就可以摆脱在说数字时候的中式英文发音。

Do these sound the same?

这些听起来一样吗？

13 (thirteen), 30 (thirty)

14 (fourteen), 40 (forty)

15 (fifteen), 50 (fifty)

16 (sixteen), 60 (sixty)

17 (seventeen), 70 (seventy)

18 (eighteen), 80 (eighty)

19 (nineteen), 90 (ninety)

Let us keep going.

11 – eleven

eleven [i **le** vvv nnn]

There is another *N* at the end of the word.

又一个以 *N* 结尾的单词。

12 – twelve; 20 – twenty

twelve [t **welll** vvv]; *twenty* [t w^nnn '**TTT**']

13 – thirteen; 30 – thirty

thirteen [thhh rrr '**TTTn**']; *thirty* [**thhh rrr** 'TTT']

There is another *N* at the end of the word.

又一个以 *N* 结尾的单词。

14 – fourteen; 40 – forty

fourteen [fff orrr '**TTTn**']; *forty* [**forrr** 'TTT']

15 – fifteen; 50 – fifty

fifteen [fff '**E**'+ye fff '**TTTn**']; *fifty* [fff '**E**'+ye fff 'TTT']

16 – sixteen; 60 – sixty

sixteen [sss 'E'+ye kkk sss '**TTTn**']; *sixty* [sss 'E'+ye kkk sss 'TTT']

17 – seventeen; 70 – seventy

seventeen [se vvv nnn '**TTTn**']; *seventy* [**se vvv nnn** 'TTT']

18 – eighteen; 80 – eighty

eighteen ['AAA' '**TTTn**']; *eighty* [**'AAA'** 'TTT']

19 – nineteen; 90 – ninety

nineteen ['nIII' n '**TTTn**']; *ninety* [**'nIII'** n 'TTT']

Between *11* and *20*, there are eight numbers that end with *N* or *Ne* (*11, 13, 14, 15, 16, 17, 18,* and *19*).

从 11 到 20，有 8 个数字都以 *N* 或 *Ne* 结尾 (11, 13, 14, 15, 16, 17, 18, 19)。

Out of the first twenty-one numbers *(0* through *20)*, twelve end with *N* or *Ne*, which is 57%. Even though many native Chinese do not pronounce *N* correctly, Americans might guess the number we are trying to say correctly—or they may not. If we say *$90* and it sounds like *$19* (that's a difference of $71), we will really confuse Americans.

前 21 个数字里 (0 到 20)，有 12 个数字都以 *N* 或 *Ne* 结尾，占了57%。

One easy way to tell the difference between *13* and *30*, *14* and *40*, and so forth, is to remember where the accent is in a word. In *13, 14,* and so on, the accent is on the second syllable. In *30, 40,* and so on, the accent is the first syllable.

有一个简单的方法来分辨/说出 13 和 30, 14 和 40 等等之间的区别，就是知道单词它的重音在哪里。

13, 14…重音在第二个音节上。

30, 40…重音在第一个音节上。

100 – *one hundred; hundred* [**h^n** dre ddd] 一百

Many native Chinese speakers omit the tail *D* sound (Principle 3).

许多中国人都会漏掉结尾 D 的音。(原则 3, 尾巴上的魔音)

1,000 – *one thousand; thousand* [thhh **auuu** zzz en ddd] 一千

Note the *Th*, the *zzz*, and the *D* sound at the end. *Thousand* is a challenging number to say.

Thousand 这个字的发音很有挑战性。*Th*, zzz 和结尾的 *D* 的发音。

10,000 – *ten thousand* 一万

Numbers are described differently in Chinese than in English. Chinese uses a unit called 万, so the equivalent of *10,000* in Chinese is 一万. I get confused when I hear 一万; I need to do a mental translation and convert 一万 to 10,000.

在表达大数字时，中文和英文用的方式不同。

在中文里有个数字的单位叫"万", 10,000 对于中国人来说是一万。当我听到"一万"的时候我得在脑子里做个转换把"一万"变成"十千"(10,000)。

1,000,000 – *one million; million* [mmm '**E**'+ye ll li nnn] 一 百万

Chinese refer to one million as 100 万. For some reason, these two units do not confuse me.

100,000,000 – *one hundred million* 一億

Chinese refer to *one hundred million* as 一億

中国人把一百个百万叫一億。

1,000,000,000 – *one billion; billion* [bbb '**E**'+**ye** ll li nnn] 十億

Chinese know *one billion* as 十億.

中国人把一千个百万叫十億。

The above is just a different way of saying the bigger numbers in English and Chinese.

Counting Money
数钱

Do these sound the same?

这些听上去一样吗?

nickel, Nicole

dime, dine

dollars, Dallas

How about the words Americans use for coins?

硬币是怎样换算的? 怎么讲呢?

A *penny* = 1 *cent*

1 便士 = 1 美分

penny [**pen** 'nEEE']

cent [sen ttt].

Many of us omit the ending *T* sound.

许多中国人都会忽略结尾 *T* 的发音。

A *nickel* = 5 *cents*

1 镍币 = 5 美分

nickel [**ni** k^ lll]

cents [sen ttt zzz].

Many of us omit the ending *T* and *S* sounds.

许多中国人都会忽略结尾 *T* 和 *S* 的发音。

A *dime* = 10 *cents*.

1 角 = 10 分

dime ['dIII' mmm]; *dime* ≠ 蛋; dime ≠ 蛋母

one dime ≠ 完蛋

A *quarter* = 25 *cents* (¼ of a dollar)

¼ 美元 = 25 美分 = 1 美元的 ¼

The word *quarter* means one-fourth of something. In coins, a *quarter* is one-fourth of a dollar.

单词 *quarter* 的意思是一个东西的四分之一。所以指硬币时，一个 *quarter* 就是一美元的 ¼。

Quarter [kw **orrr** terrr]

A dollar = 100 cents = 20 nickels = 10 dimes = 4 quarters

1 美元 = 100 美分 = 20 镍币 = 10 角 = 4 个 25 美分

Phone numbers
电话号码

U.S. phone numbers have ten digits: (xxx) yyy-zzzz

美国的电话号码有十位数: (xxx)yyy-zzzz。

The first three, xxx, refer to an area code. The seven-digit phone number is yyy-zzzz.

其中 xxx 是区号, yyy-zzzz 是 7 位电话号码。

If you look at a phone pad, you will see it has ten numbers, plus two symbols: * (star) and # (pound). Many native Chinese speakers do not say *star* or *pound*. Many Chinese say * 星 (*star* in Chinese). To further confuse matters, the *star* symbol looks like Chinese writing; it is similar to the Chinese pictogram for 米 (*rice*). The *pound* symbol is similar to the Chinese pictogram for 井 (*well*).

如果你看一下手机键盘, 除了十个数字之外, 还有 * 和 # 两个符号。很多中国人说 * "星" (star 的中文) 或 "米" (类似中文), 说 # "井" (类似中文)。

* = star

= pound

My office's phone number is (626) 584-9999. To share my phone number in conversation, normally I would say only the seven-digit phone number: "five eight four, nine nine nine nine" or "five eight four, ninety-nine ninety-nine."

If the other party asks for the area code, then I would say, "Area code six two six."

我的办公室电话号码是（626）584-9999，我通常只会说 7 位数的电话号码: "five eight four, nine, nine, nine, nine 5, 8, 4, 9, 9, 9, 9 " 或者 "five eight four, ninety-nine, ninety-nine 5, 8, 4, 99, 99"。

如果对方问我区号,那么我会说 "区号是" "six two six 6, 2, 6"。

U.S. zip codes
美国邮编

Generally, U.S. zip codes have five digits, although they can have up to nine digits.

美国的邮编通常是 5 位数, 但是也会多达 9 位数。

When speaking, many Americans replace the number *zero* with the letter *O*. This is just idiomatic slang—a fact to be memorized, not scrutinized. For example, *90210* is one of the zip codes for Beverly Hills. Instead of saying, "*Nine zero two one zero*," you could say, "*Nine O two one O*."

许多美国人把数字 "0" (zero) 用字母 *O* 代替。

举例来说: 90210 是加州比佛利山庄的其中一个邮编, 可以说 "nine zero two one zero", 亦可以说 "nine O two one O"。

Credit card numbers
信用卡号码

Just giving your credit card information in English over the phone presents native Chinese with many challenges.

仅仅是通过电话提供你的信用卡信息, 就存在许多的挑战。

At the front of the card, you have:

- The name of the card (*Visa, MasterCard*, etc.)
- A 16-digit credit card number (a group of four four-digit numbers).
- An expiration date
- The name of the cardholder

On the back of the card, there is a three-digit security code.

卡的正面有:

- 卡的名称 (Visa, MasterCard 等等)
- 一个 16 位的卡号 (4 个 4 位数的组合)

- 一个过期日
- 卡上的名字 (你的姓名)

卡的背面, 有一个 3 位数的安全码。

Visa [**'vEEE'** s^]

MasterCard [mmm **e** sss terrr k 'RRR' ddd]

expiration ['XXX' pe **'rAAA'** shhh ^ nnn]

security ['CCC' **'QQQ'** ri 'TTT']

date ['dAAA' ttt]

If this proves too difficult, you might say, "I do not give credit card information over the phone; I use my PC to enter the information." However, once in a while you may be forced to provide this information over the phone, such as when you call your bank or a merchant. This has happened to me several times.

也许你会说 "我不会通过电话提供我的信用卡信息, 我用电脑输入信息"。我同意。然而, 偶尔总会有被逼无奈通过电话提供你的信息, 比如你打银行的 800 号电话的时候或者打给某家商户的时候。这类情况在我身上发生过很多次。

Let's try a sample expiration date: *05/2013*.

You have several options for reading this date aloud.

For *05*: *May*; *zero five*; *five*; *O five*.

For *2013*: *two thousand thirteen*; *thirteen*; *twenty thirteen*; *one three*

So, for *05/2013*, we have:

- *Zero five one three*

- *Five one three* (It is easier to say the letter *O* for *0* than to say the word *zero* because of the combined difficulty of the *Z* and *R* sounds.)
- *O five one three*
- *O five thirteen.*

以有效期 05/2013 为例，有好几种讲法:

05: "May"; "zero five"; "five"; "O five"。

2013: "two thousand thirteen"; "thirteen"; "twenty thirteen"; "one three"。

所以，05/2013，我们就有:

- "zero five one three",
- "O five one three", (在说数字 0 的时候，因为 *Z* 和 *R* 的发音，用字母 O 比用单词 "zero" 更简单)。
- "O" five thirteen,
- "five thirteen"。

Which one should you pick and say? I pick the last one. It is short and easy for the listener to understand correctly. Even if your pronunciation of *13* sounds like *30*, the number *30* (referring to *2030*) would not show on a credit card until several years from now. Thus, the other party will write down the number *13*.

到底选择哪个来表达呢? 我选择最后一个。它很短，对于电话那头的另一方来说又很容易就记下正确的数字。即使你的数字 13 的发音听上去像 30，但由于数字 30 对于现在来说，2030 年不太可能，对方就会写下数字 13。

CHAPTER 15

第十五章

The End is Near: Are We Doing Much Better?

快谢幕了，是否有很大的进步呢？

What's Next?

下一步呢？

How are we doing? By now, we have reviewed all sixteen letters in the English alphabet that are new to native Chinese speakers; we have also reviewed 30 sound choices for the five vowels (*A, E, I, O,* and *U*). Some are extremely easy and some are quite challenging. No matter what, I hope you have realized the importance of correct English pronunciation.

到现在为止，我们已经把英文字母表中，16 个对于中国人来说是新的字母音回顾了一遍；同时我们也讲了五个元音 (*A, E, I, O,* and *U*) 的 30 种发音选择。有些字母音非常简单，而有些字母音非常有挑战性。无论如何，希望你能意识到正确的英语发音的重要性。

Once you have learned to pronounce these sounds the right way and to make the correct choices about sounds in the words you are saying, you can bring your English speaking up to a much higher level.

一旦你学会了正确的发这些音的方式，也学会为你正在说的单词选择正确的发音，你的英语口语就更上一层楼了!

At the beginning of the book, I suggested you record yourself saying the alphabet and the first several numbers up to ten. After you are done with this book, make that same recording again. Then, compare your pronunciation. I hope you will hear a dramatic difference between the "before" and "after."

在本书伊始，我建议你把自己读字母表 (A – Z) 和 0 到 10 为止的 11 个数字的音录下来。读完本书之后，再录一遍。然后对比一下你自己的发音。希望你能听出"之前"和"之后"的巨大差异。

Are we done yet?

我们到此为止了吗?

Yes and no. This depends on what you want. If you are happy with where you are in the stages of learning proper English speaking, and if you have made enough progress by going through the book, then congratulations! I am happy for you, and I am very glad that I have been able to help you to speak better English. Thank you.

既是，也不是。这取决于你想要什么。如果你已满足于你所处的英语阶段能学到的一些英语口语，而且通过对本书的学习，你已取得很大的进步，那么恭喜你! 我为你感到高兴，同时也为我能帮助你讲更好的英文而开心。谢谢。

What if you are asking, "What's next?" Well, we have just started our journey. Please check www.66English.com for further information and for instructions about the best way to get into a language-learning environment (Principle 6).

Thank you and see you soon!

如果你问 "接下来呢?" 这段旅程我们才刚刚开始。请浏览网站 www.66english.com 以获得更多的资讯, 以及有关如何融入一个语言学习與交流环境的信息. 谢谢! 希望能有与你网上相见或面对面的交流机会!

- 16 New Sounds for Chinese Speakers Derived from the Twenty-Six Letters
- The 66English_{SM} Pronunciation Key System

16 New Sounds For Chinese Speakers

A	B	**C**	D	E	**F**	**G**	3
H	I	**J**	**K**				3
L	**M**	**N**	O	P			3
Q	**R**	**S**	T	U	**V**		4
W	**X**	Y	**Z**				3
							16

Out of 26 letters (A-Z), 16 are new for Chinese speakers 16/26 = 62%

66English_{SM} Pronunciation Key System
溜溜英语发音体系
www.66english.com

The "66English_{SM} Pronunciation Key System" uses the 26 letters of the English alphabet (A-Z) along with an additional symbol ^. No more confusing symbols (ʒ, ʊ, æ, ŋ, ʃ, θ, etc.) to learn or to remember.

Just a few simple rules:

- Three letters in a pronunciation key indicate drawing out the sound. For example, 'AAA' sounds just like the letter 'A' with a longer sound. The Chinese tend to make their English letter sounds short and abrupt. Example: ace ['AAA' sss]

- ^ is pronounced as a very short "ah" sound. Example: bus [b^ sss]

- See chapter 2 for the pronunciation of this mysterious *i* sound. Example: b*i*t [b 'E'+ye ttt]

- Use simple and easy to pronounce one syllable words to show new pronunciation. Example: base ["bay" sss] or ['bAAA' sss]

- An accent of a word is shown in **bolded** letters. Example: China [chhh '**III**' n^]

205

"溜溜英语发音体系" 建立在:

1) 英文字母表中的 26 个字母和一个符号 ^ 。不需再用那些让人搞不清楚的符号 (ʒ, ʊ, æ, ŋ, ʃ, θ , 等等)。

2) 一些简单的规则。

- 二个或三个相同的字母表示要发一个长音。比如 'AAA' 表示发一个长音 "A"。中国人往往把英文字母的发音发的很短促。举例: ace ['AAA' sss]

- ^ 代表一个很短的 "ah" 音。举例: bus [b^ sss]

- 神秘的 *i* 的发音, 请见第二章。举例: bit [b 'E'+ye ttt]

- 使用简洁的单音节单词米展示发音。举例: base ["bay" sss] or ['bAAA' sss]

- 单词的重音用黑体字表示。举例: China [chhh '**III**' n^]

The 5 Vowels (A, E, I, O, U)
5 个元音

		Letter 元音	Example(s) 例子	66English_{SM} Pronunciation Key 溜溜英语发音	Sounds like 听起来像
1	1	a	<u>a</u>pe ['AAA' ppp], <u>a</u>ce ['AAA' sss]	'AAA'	letter 'A'
2	2	a	b<u>a</u>d [bbb a ddd], <u>a</u>t [a ttt]	a	a
3	3	a	b<u>a</u>r [bbb ahhh 'RRR']	ahhh	ah
4	4	a	<u>a</u>ll [awww lll], s<u>a</u>w [sss awww]	awww	aw
5	5	a	ag<u>a</u>in [^ **ggg e nnn**]	e	e
6	6	a	or<u>a</u>nge [**awww rin jjj**]	i	i
7	7	a	Chin<u>a</u> [**chhh 'III' n^**], ag<u>a</u>in [^ **ggg e nnn**]	^	^
8	8	a	pe<u>a</u> ['PPP'], bo<u>a</u>t ['bOOO' ttt]	---	silence
9	1	e	sh<u>e</u> [shhh 'EEE']	'EEE'	letter 'E'
10	2	e	b<u>e</u>d [bbb e ddd]	e	e
11	3	e	int<u>e</u>rest ['E'+**ye** n ter ris ttt]	i	i
12	4	e	b<u>e</u>ta ["bay" t^] or ['bAAA' t^]	'AAA'	letter 'A'
13	5	e	ap<u>e</u> ['AAA' ppp], hom<u>e</u> ['hOOO' mmm]	---	silence

14	1	i	ice ['eye' sss], or ['III' sss]	'III'	letter 'I'
15	2	i	Lisa ['IEEE' s^]	'EEE'	letter 'E'
16	3	i	it ['E'+ye ttt]	'E'+ye	i (unique)
17	4	i	mini [mi 'nEEE']	i	i
18	5	i	business [b 'E'+ye zzz ni zzz]	---	silence
19	1	o	oat ['OOO' ttt], coke ['kOOO' kkk]	'OOO'	letter 'O'
20	2	o	box [b ahhh kkk sss]	ahhh	ah
21	3	o	dog [d awww ggg]	awww	aw
22	4	o	love [l^ vvv], son [sss ^ nnn]	^	^
23	5	o	woman [www u mmm ^ nnn]	u	u
24	6	o	opossum [p ahhh s^ mmm]	---	slience
25	1	u	you ['UUU']	'UUU'	letter 'U'
26	2	u	yogurt ["you" gerrr ttt]	e	e
27	3	u	minute [mi ni ttt]	i	i
28	4	u	cut [kkk ^ ttt], sun [sss ^ nnn]	^	^
29	5	u	tube [tuuu bbb]	uuu	u
30	6	u	laugh [lll aaa fff]	---	silence

There are *at least* 30 sound choices for these 5 vowels.

- The 'A' has at least 8 sounds to choose from.
- The 'E' has at least 5 sounds to choose from.
- The 'I' has at least 5 sounds to choose from.

- The 'O' has at least 6 sounds to choose from.
- The 'U' has at least 6 sounds to choose from.

5 个元音 (A, E, I, O, U) 至少有 30 种发音可选。
- "A" 至少有 8 种发音可选。
- "E" 至少有 5 种发音可选。
- "I" 至少有 5 种发音可选。
- "O" 至少有 6 种发音可选。
- "U" 至少有 6 种发音可选。

The 21 Consonants
21 个辅音

		Letter 辅音	Examples 例子	66English_{SM} Pronunciation Key 溜溜英语发音	Sounds like 听起来像
1	1	b	bed [bbb e ddd], Bob [bbb ahhh bbb]	bbb	b (airy sound)
2	2	b	dumb [d^ mmm], comb ['kOOO' mmm]	---	silence
3	1	c	cider ['sIII' derrr], cent [sen ttt]	sss	s (airy sound)
4	2	c	cry [kkk 'rIII'], cola ['kOOO' laaa]	kkk	k (airy sound)
5	3	c	black [bl aa kkk]	---	silence
6	1	d	deed ['DDD' ddd]	ddd	d (airy sound)
7	2	d	fudge [fff ^ jjj]	---	silence
8	1	f	fee ['fEEE'], if ['E'+ye fff}	fff	f (airy sound)
9	1	g	go ['gOOO']	ggg	g (airy sound)
10	2	g	page ["pay" jjj]	jjj	j (airy sound)
11	3	g	sign ['sIII' nnn]	---	silence
12	1	h	he ['hEEE']	hhh	h (airy sound)
13	2	h	hour [auuu wrrr]	---	silence

14	1	j	jet [jjj e ttt]	jjj	j (airy sound)
15	1	k	ca<u>k</u>e ['KKK' kkk]	kkk	k (airy sound)
16	2	k	<u>k</u>nee ['nEEE']	---	silence
17	1	l	a<u>ll</u> [awww lll], <u>l</u>et [le ttt]	lll	l (airy sound)
18	2	l	wou<u>l</u>d [w^uuu ddd]	---	silence
19	1	m	<u>m</u>o<u>m</u> [mmm **ahhh** mmm]	mmm	m (airy sound)
20	2	m	<u>m</u>nemonics [ni **mon** ni kkk sss]	---	silence
21	1	n	<u>n</u>o ['nOOO']	nnn	n (airy sound)
22	2	n	colum<u>n</u> [kaww l^ mmm]	---	silence
23	1	p	a<u>p</u>e ['AAA' ppp]	ppp	p (airy sound)
24	2	p	recei<u>p</u>t [ri "seat"]	---	silence
25	1	q	Ira<u>q</u> ['EEE' **rahhh** kkk] or ['EEE **rock**"]	kkk	k (airy sound)
26	1	r	a<u>r</u>t ['RRR' ttt]	'RRR'	letter 'R'
27	2	r	<u>r</u>ed [rrr e ddd]	rrr	r (airy sound)
28	1	s	<u>s</u>on = <u>s</u>un [sss ^ nnn]	sss	s (airy sound)
29	2	s	mu<u>s</u>ic [**mmm** 'UUU' zzz 'E'+ye kkk]	zzz	z
30	3	s	ai<u>s</u>le ['III' lll] or ["eye" lll]	---	silence
31	1	t	ea<u>t</u> ['EEE' ttt]	ttt	t (airy sound)

32	2	t	patien_t_ ["**pay**" shhh ^n ttt]	shhh	sh (airy sound)
33	3	t	depo_t_ ['DDD' 'pOOO']	---	silence
34	1	v	_v_ery [vvv e 'rEEE']	vvv	v (airy sound)
35	1	w	_w_e [www 'EEE']	www	w (airy sound)
36	2	w	ans_w_er [**annn** serrr]	---	silence
37	1	x	e_x_cuse [i ks 'QQQ' zzz]	ks	ks
38	1	y	_y_es [ye sss]	y	y (airy sound)
39	2	y	cr_y_ [kkk 'rIII']	'III'	letter 'I'
40	1	z	_z_oo [zuuu]	zzz	z

There are *at least* 40 sound choices for these 21 consonants (21 = 26 letters (A-Z) - 5 vowels (A, E, I, O, U)).

There are at least a total of 70 sound choices for all 26 A-Z letters (30 for the A, E, I, O, U vowels and 40 for the remaining consonants).

从 A 到 Z 的 26 个字母里, 一共至少有 70 种发音可选 (元音 A, E, I, O, U 至少有 30 种, 剩下的辅音至少有 40 种)。

The development of this system is an ongoing process. Please refer to www.66English.com for the latest updates.

溜溜英语发音体系仍在持续不断的拓展中。请访问我们的网站 www.66English.com 以获取最新资讯。

关于作者

Kenneth Ma 马一飞 (馬一飛) was born in Taiwan and came to the United States as a graduate student when he was twenty-six years old. He has been living in Los Angeles, California, for thirty-plus years. His academic background is in electronic hardware and computer software engineering. Today he and his wife lead a real estate settlement services (escrow) company in the Los Angeles area.

当今世界, 复杂的社会关系赋予了每个人多重个性和角色。若遵从惯例, 这本书的作者介绍应该这样开始:

马一飞, 英文名 Kenneth Ma, 19XX 年生于台湾, 毕业于美国南加州大学 (University of Southern California) 计算机科学系 (Computer Science), 获硕士学位 (M.S.), 是最早一批接触 计算机的IT业者。19XX 年起, 他与太太一起在加州洛杉矶经营一家房地产 escrow 公司, 至今已十五年有余⋯⋯

看似中规中矩, 但作为一个 "好奇的读者", 你一定会说: 请问这跟本书有什么关系?

Although a top student in his English classes in Taiwan, he found that he was unable to properly communicate with the Americans he met in his junior year in college. The English teaching system taught students how to pass tests but did not put any emphasis on actual communication. As there were very few Americans in Taiwan at that time the actual speaking of English outside of the classroom was rare.

Since then, he started his long and lonely journey to improve his English speaking skills.

爱音乐的理工男，不甘心的英语高材生

处在计算机有关的"工程圈"中心，Ken 的"不一样"在于他有个"文艺青年"的爱好，就是音乐，尤其是美式摇滚音乐。

兴趣是最好的老师，对音乐的着迷让 Ken 对声音极其敏感，在没有正式学过音乐，也看不懂五线谱的情况下，他不仅学会了弹吉他和电子琴，更对英文课情有独钟，从初中，高中直到大学，他的英文成绩一路领先。

大三升大四那年的暑假，他参加了台北女青年会 (YWCA) 主办的英语夏令营，也结识了很多来自美国的年轻的指导员。尽管夏令营里的美国指导员会刻意放慢语速与台湾同学交谈，彼此之间还是有许多沟通不畅，之前在学校里学的很多单词和句型派不上用场。

英语交流越是不畅，就越是令 Ken 感到不安，甚至发展成了不甘心。自己的英文基础不是很好吗? 怎么"真刀真枪"地同老外交谈却不行了? 他开始不满足于英文课上取得的优秀成绩，而发自内心地意识到交谈畅通，沟通顺利才是学习一门语言的真正目的。这样，练好英语口语就成了他想要赢得的一场比赛，而对手，就是自己。

By immersing himself in the English speaking environment whenever possible—speaking English at work, at home, with friends—his speaking skills have steadily improved. He developed the 66English system and it has worked for him and his students.

ABC 口语世界里 的 "独自漂流"

夏令营后不久, Ken 开始了一个人的英语口语学习。那是一个孤独漫长的过程。说孤独, 是因为没有老师, 也没有一起研究的同伴, 他只能通过日常与美国人交流, 仔细观看和倾听他们的发音与口型, 舍弃音标, 单纯的去模仿。说漫长, 是因为每个字母、单词都没有现成的方法可以借鉴, 一个简单的字母i的发音让他花费了 3 个月时间去练习和总结, 然后再在与人交流的过程中完善。

1975 年, Ken 前往美国攻读计算机工程硕士学位。求学阶段, 他在学校的计算机室打工, 工作中最有挑战的部分是接电话, 尤其是记录电话号码, 每次他都需要在大脑中将数字进行一番 "中英文转换"。

当时的洛杉矶, 华人比现在少很多, 但这也给了 Ken 良好的英语练习环境, 使他在学习和工作阶段不得不努力练习英文。当然, 他也得到了很多人的帮助。

首先, Ken 毕业后一直在美国公司工作, 同事都是美国人, 老板、上司和同事也都成了 Ken 模仿、练习口语的对象。

其次是他的太太, Ken 的太太同样来自台湾, 因为家庭背景的关系, 她的母语是英文, 英语好过国语, 这样 Ken 有了一个练习英语的最大优势——家庭环境。

第三, Ken 到了美国后, 仍然没有放弃自己对音乐的痴迷, 业余时间他还在继续找人一起交流、学习弹吉他, 玩音乐。他的美国老师们指出了他很多英语口语上需要改进的地方。

最后, 他身边的同学、朋友, 都给了 Ken 很多英语口语方面的灵感和启发。

工作环境 + 家庭环境 + 音乐环境 + 交友环境——这些生活环境就是 Ken 持续练习口语的最大动力。那个不甘心的

Ken, 因为环境而坚持不懈地练习口语, 最终将所有心得汇集成了一套经验总结: 66 (溜溜) 英语口语系统。

66 (溜溜) 英语: 个性化的创新英语口语学习系统

毫无疑问, 尽管得到了这么多人的帮助, 但 66 (溜溜) 英语口语的演化还是要归功于那个孤独而漫长的过程。但孤独令人自由, 漫长使人审慎, 自由和审慎使 Ken 得以抛弃常规, 违反传统, 总结一套全新的发音系统。

Ken 的成功还要感谢他那双对声音极其敏感的耳朵。凭借这双耳朵, 他总结出: 26 个英文字母的地道发音, 其实没有一个可以与中文发音相对应; 而传统音标, 几乎是完全可以抛弃不用的; 要改正说英语时的中文口音, 可以试着把句子像唱歌一样说出来; **要说地道英语, 你不需要加快语速, 反而是要放慢, 发好每一个音……**

而且, 为求标准且便于记忆, Ken 创新地把英文发音和汉字进行组合, 并尝试利用嘴型和舌头的位置来达成发音效果, 这些个人总结完全与传统教学无关, 甚至有些地方存在矛盾, 但效果异常明显。

也许你要问 Ken, 66 (溜溜) 英语的研究和开发到目前为止结束了吗? 这个过程有多长呢?

Ken 说, 从他开始练习英语口语至今, 已经过去了 40 多年的光阴, 他的系统都会更新, 永无停止。口语是与人类日常生活最紧密相关的文化, 它随时间潮流而动, 每时每刻都有新的单词和句型涌现。**66 (溜溜) 英语随时注意口语发展的新动向, 注意搜罗记录英语口语中出现的新鲜词汇, 所以可以永保鲜活。**

分享一个 "活着" 的 66 (溜溜) 英语口语

回顾几十年来的学习与总结, Ken 觉得非常充实, 他从 66 (溜溜) 英语口语中获益匪浅, 无论工作还是生活都因流利而地道的英语而加分。现在, 他的主要任务在于分享。Ken 会讲流利的英语但不等于他会教。他从十多年前开始着手研究分享 66 (溜溜) 英语的方法, 通过一批定期上课的学生, 教学相长, 他从交互式的交流中不断改进分享的方法。

There has been a huge influx of young Chinese coming to the States to continue with their higher education. These students are facing the same problems that Ken faced many years ago, particularly those who live in the heavily Chinese populated cities such as Los Angeles, San Francisco, New York, etc. Many of these Chinese have come to realize that with the shrinking boundaries of the world, perfectly spoken English has become a very important tool to be used at school and at work whether in the United States or in China.

近些年, 在美国的中国留学生渐渐成为一个广泛的群体。但困难却因口语较差接踵而至: 大多数留学生在国内都是学业成绩很好, 英文成绩更是名列前茅, 但口语却因为缺乏一定的语言环境和正确指导而差强人意。很多中国留学生在美国学习的专业是会计 (Accounting), 财经 (Finance), 工程 (Engineering), 在某些学校, 会计专业的硕士课程居然有 90% 是中国留学生, 很大一部分原因在于这类课程不需要太多的语言交流。而像 市场 (Marketing), 法律 (Law), MBA 等课程则相对少有中国学生问津。如果能帮助中国的学生练就一口流利地道的英语口语, 对于他们的学业拓展乃至融入美国社会或是回国发展都是非常有帮助的。

在中国与世界联系愈发紧密的今天, 流利的英语口语对哪怕不打算迈出国门的中国人同样重要。例如, 目前美国本土的很多大企业都倾向于将电话客服的服务外包,承接者大多来自印度或菲律宾等国家的公司。客服服务相对简单轻松,但由于需要英语交流,几乎没有中国公司涉及。难道聪明的中国人只能做"沉默的大多数"吗?随着成为全球第二大经济体,是时候让我们在国际舞台上发声了。

This book is the culmination of many years of effort. In it, the author shares the methods and experiences that have worked for him and other Chinese. This is a book that he has wanted to write for the last eleven years; and with its publication, he will finally be able to share what he knows.

这本酝酿 11 年有余的书,是 Ken 多年不懈努力的结晶和写照,包含对 Ken 本人乃至全体中国人都有效的方法和经验,但其含义远远超出一本书和教材的范畴。**随着本书的出版,Ken 更希望在读者中掀起一股学习英语口语的热潮,让我们的英语教育更加重视真正的实用英语口语导向,才是此书出版的真正目的。**

August, 2013

2013 年 8 月

www.66English.com

Printed in the USA
CPSIA information can be obtained
at www.ICGtesting.com
JSHW012050140824
68134JS00035B/3359

9 781599 323541